HOW TO CLAIM S

In this Series

other titles in preparation

How To Books General Editor Roland Seymour

How To...

CLAIM STATE BENEFITS

Martin Rathfelder

Northcote House

First published 1987
Second Edition 1988

© *Copyright 1988 by Martin Rathfelder*

First published in 1988 by Northcote House Publishers Ltd., Harper
& Row House, Estover Road, Plymouth PL6 7PZ, United Kingdom.
Tel: Plymouth (0752) 705251. Telex: 45635.

British Library Cataloguing in Publication Data
Rathfelder, Martin, 1952-
    How to claim state benefits. — 2nd ed. —
    (How to books).
    1. Great Britain. Welfare benefits.
    Claims — Manuals
    I. Title
    361.6'0941

    ISBN 0-7463-0531-1

Printed and bound in Great Britain by
Biddles Ltd, Guildford and King's Lynn

Contents

I have relied heavily on my colleagues in the Manchester City Council Welfare Rights Service in preparing this second edition, particularly Paul Cassidy, Tudor Owen, David Singer, Ian Ford, Dympna O'Dowd, Clive Martin, Kathy Brooks, Marian Simmonds and Terry Patterson.

This book is dedicated to Emily Lawrence, in spite of whom it was written.

What this book is about

This book is a simple guide to the social security system, with a few notes on taxation and other matters which affect claimants. It is mostly concerned with the problems of poorer people, although many of the things mentioned affect everyone.

How to use it

The articles are set out in alphabetical order. If you look up the wrong title there should be a message to tell you which article to look at. The names of articles you should look up for more details about a point are given in **bold** type.

There are articles on:

● each benefit that you can claim
● different groups of people
● problem areas not limited to any one group of people, like **rent, fuel, income tax**
● special words that are used in other articles, like **non-dependant**

Where to begin

If you are not sure where to begin choose one of the articles about people first. They are:

babies, boarders, children, death, disabled, employed, homeless, immigrants, prisoners, retired, self-employed, sick, single parents, strikers, students, unemployed, widows, women.

Most of the benefits are administered by the **DHSS,** and if you have trouble getting them you should read that article.

Limitations on the book

The law on social security changes very quickly. This book is intended to be correct as in April 1988, but the details of some of the changes which will take effect on that date had not been announced when it was written. Major changes in **means-tested** benefits come into effect on that date, and the information in the book is based on what the Government had announced in February 1988. There may be changes between the time of writing and the time you read the information, for instance, in the Budget. If you need to be certain get **advice.** I have mentioned some of the changes which the Government intend to introduce, where there are enough details, but plans often change as they get nearer to reality.

The benefits described in the book operate in England and Wales. I have not tried to describe any local benefits. For those you would need to contact your local Council. Almost all the benefits will be the same in Scotland, and I have indicated where there is a difference. Northern Ireland has a separate but similar benefit system and I have not stated where there are differences. The Isle of Man and the Channel Islands do not have the same system of benefits at all.

As this is only a beginner's book I have had to simplify everything and leave out lots of complications. I have tried to mention all the benefits which you can claim now, but I have not put in any details of benefits which have been abolished, although there are still lots of people getting them. In particular, if you were on Supplementary Benefit until it was abolished you should benefit from **Transitional Protection.** This means that you shouldn't get any less on **Income Support** than you did on Supplementary Benefit.

If you find the information in the book is not enough to sort out your problem go to the heading **Advice** to find out where to get more information. If you want more details of any of the general books referred to in the articles then see the heading **Books.**

Abroad

The rules for each benefit on what happens if you go abroad are listed under the name of the benefit. The rules on whether you are entitled if you have just come from abroad are also listed, under 'Residence Requirements'. For more details about this *see also* **Immigrants.**

Where is abroad?
Abroad includes Northern Ireland and the Isle of Man, technically, but in fact you will not lose any benefit by moving from or to those places. The Channel Islands, however, have their own social security system, but if you are entitled to a United Kingdom benefit you are not disqualified just because you are in the Channel Islands.

There are special rules for civil servants, mariners, crews of civil aircraft, and members of the forces serving abroad.

European Community
There are special rules for people who move around within the European Community, because the law of the Community overrules the laws of each individual country. If you have paid contributions in another member country you should be able to claim benefits in this country. It is very slow for the benefit you have earned abroad to come through. Your claim will be sent from the local **DHSS** to the Overseas branch, Newcastle upon Tyne, NE98 1YX and from there to the country where your contributions were paid. It sometimes takes up to a year for any benefit to arrive, so you may have to claim **Income Support** until it is sorted out.

The European Community includes Belgium, Denmark, France, West Germany, Greece, Ireland, Italy, Luxemburg, Netherlands, Portugal, Spain, United Kingdom and Gibraltar.

The Overseas branch will send you leaflets about the position if you write to them:

EC Guide no 1 for people going to work in another member country. There is a separate edition for each country. The United Kingdom edition deals with Gibraltar and also tells you how to claim British benefits while you are abroad.

EC Guide no 2 for temporary stays in another member country deals with rights to medical treatment on holiday etc. Leaflet SA 30 from your local **DHSS** has similar information.

EC Guide no 3 for people sent by an employer in the UK to work in another member country.

EC Guide no 4 for pensioners in one country who are entitled to benefit from another.

EC Guide no 5 for people who depend on a person who works in another member country.

Reciprocal arrangements

If there is a reciprocal arrangement with a country then you can get benefits which are covered by the arrangement while you are in that particular country, and people from there can claim here. You can get a leaflet about the arrangements for each country from the Overseas branch. The countries covered are:

Australia, Austria, Bermuda, Canada, Cyprus, Finland, Iceland, Israel, Jamaica, Jersey and Guernsey, Malta, Mauritius, New Zealand, Norway, Sweden, Switzerland, Turkey, USA, Yugoslavia.

Leaflets

There is a general leaflet about social security abroad (NI 38) and a general leaflet about the EEC (SA 29). If you are just going abroad for a holiday you need to know about medical costs abroad. Get leaflet SA 30. This includes an application for a certificate to entitle you to free medical treatment in the EEC.

Getting benefit abroad

If you go abroad and you are entitled to one of the benefits which can continue while you are abroad you will have to decide how you want to be paid. There are four possibilities:

1. You keep your order book and cash the orders when you get back. Each order can be cashed within three months of its date.
2. The **DHSS** pay the money into your bank account, or to someone else for you.
3. You can authorise someone else to cash your order book.
4. The **DHSS** can pay you while you are abroad. They will usually pay you through a particular bank.

You should arrange what you want to do before you go. **Child Benefit, One Parent Benefit,** and **Invalid Care Allowance** cannot be paid using method 4.

Absence from home	*see* **Housing Benefit** **Owner Occupiers**

Accidents at work	*see* **Industrial Benefits**

Adaptations	*see* **Disabled** **Owner Occupiers**

Additional component	*see* **National Insurance**

Advice

This is only a simple guide. If your problem is in any way unusual or complicated, or just beyond the scope of this book then you should get more information or advice.

You can get advice from **books** or from people. You may need to find out more about your problem before you can decide which books or organisations you need. This is a list of organisations which deal with general questions. Organisations which deal mainly with particular problems are dealt with in the part of the book which deals with that problem.

Where to get advice:

● Libraries

Even if you don't want a book the library can be helpful. Most of them have lists of local organisations and what they do and some have special collections of community information, perhaps with a community librarian to run them. The only point to watch is that sometimes the information they have is a bit out-of-date. Most of the books mentioned will be in main libraries, and a branch library will be able to get them for you. Make sure that you get an up-to-date edition. The Government has changed the law a lot in the last few years.

● Citizens' Advice Bureaux (CABx)

Look up your nearest one in the telephone book. They are free, independent, impartial and confidential. Often they are overstretched, too. You may have to wait for an hour or two to be seen, especially if you go at the wrong time. Usually Monday mornings are very busy, so go later in the week if you can. The sort of service you will get varies from place to place, and even from time to time, because most of the workers are volunteers and only work one day per week. They all have an excellent information system which is kept up-to-date every month and they are also very good at finding out obscure information. Some Bureaux will take on your case and represent you at an **appeal** if you want them to.

● Solicitors

There are even more solicitors than CABx and they are even more variable. All the problems mentioned in this book are basically legal problems, but not all solicitors look on them that way. Some specialise in social security and others seem to think of it as beneath them. If you are planning to ask a solicitor for help you should try to find out how much of this sort of work the solicitor has done recently. Solicitors in the country, where they are expected to deal with everything, and those in the poorer parts of cities, are more likely to know about these problems than solicitors who earn their living selling houses or dealing with business problems. Some solicitors even employ welfare rights officers who specialise in social security problems.

Solicitors are in business and need to be paid for their work. If you are poor enough you may qualify for **legal aid.** If you are not sure if you qualify for that you can ask for a £5 fixed fee interview. For that you get up to half an hour's advice. **Legal aid** will not pay for the solicitor to appear for you at an **appeal,** but it might pay for the preparation of documents to support your case.

Lists of all the solicitors in an area are held in the Solicitors' Regional Directory which will be kept by the library and the CAB. It also has details of what sort of work the firms of solicitors deal with.

● Law Centres

Law Centres specialise in the sort of problems poorer people face. They usually do a lot of work on housing, social security, employment, and immigration. Because they are often very busy it may not be easy to see someone there. Most law centres are in large cities.

● Independent Advice Centres

There is a wide variety of independent advice centres, particularly in cities. They vary a great deal. If there is one near you the only way in which you could tell if it would help you is by trying it out.

● **DHSS**

Local **DHSS** offices are not very reliable places to get advice. The staff on the counter are often junior and inexperienced. They are also very busy. Some of them are not impartial. If you only want to know something straightforward they should be able to help you, but if it is complicated or you are very worried it might be better to go to somewhere else.

If you really need to know what the **DHSS** think about a problem it may be better to write to them. If it is important the letter should be checked by somebody senior and the advice be more reliable than the counter staff give you. There is a national FREEPHONE service. Dial 0800 666 555, you will not have to pay for the call. The staff will give general advice about any sort of benefit, but they will not know about your individual case because they will not have your papers there. *See* **DHSS.**

● Social Services

Some social workers will help with benefit problems. Some of them are very good, but others seem to think that money problems are not important enough for them to get involved in. They are more likely to get involved if you are old, or ill, or have young children.

Some social services offices have specialist welfare rights officers who will help with any benefit problem.

● Probation

Probation officers are often quite interested and expert in benefit problems. You can only go to them for help if you have been in trouble with the police at some time.

● Members of Parliament

Most MPs hold surgeries in their constituencies to deal with problems people bring to them. They can be very useful, both because a letter from an MP usually gets a quick answer out of any bureaucrat and also because some MPs actually think about the problems they see in their surgeries and bear them in mind when they make decisions in Parliament. If you think that you are suffering because of some general fault in the system then make sure your MP knows about it.

If you are suffering from delay and inaction from a government department then an MP is usually your best remedy. If your MP thinks your problem is serious s/he will write to the Minister about it. The Minister's office will get in touch with the local manager, and the manager will be round to the desk of the responsible person the same day to see why his/her prospects of promotion are being spoiled.

It's usually best to write to your MP at the House of Commons, London SW1A 0AA, because then the MP can pass your letter on to the Minister directly, without having to write down all the details.

● Ombudsman

If you think you have suffered because of maladministration then you can ask the Ombudsman to investigate. Ombudsmen are employed to help people who have suffered from ill treatment by officials. Maladministration means that the way a decision was made was bad, not just that you disagreed with it.

What can the Ombudsman investigate?

● failure to reply to letters quickly and properly
● giving misleading or inaccurate advice
● rudeness, bias, discrimination or inconsistency
● failure to have proper ways of doing things, or failure to follow the rules

If you think that you have suffered in this way because of a Government Department you must write to your MP and ask for the Ombudsman to investigate. The MP must pass your complaint on. You should give full details in your letter.

Warning. The Ombudsman is usually very thorough, but very slow. The Ombudsman is not much help in sorting out an urgent problem which is still going on. It is a good way of getting an apology, and sometimes extra payments, if you have suffered in the past through maladministration.

You can get more details from The Parliamentary Ombudsman, Church House, Great Smith Street, London SW1P 3BW.

There is a separate Ombudsman for the Health Service who can investigate what services are provided by the Health Service and how they work, as well as delay, rudeness and mistakes. You must write first to the health authority, and if you are not satisfied with their answer write direct to the Health Service Ombudsman, Church House, Great Smith Street, London SW1P 3BW. He cannot investigate complaints against family doctors, dentists or opticians.

● Councillors

Councillors can be useful allies if you are in trouble. They are most effective in dealing with your local council, but some of them will tackle other organisations as well. They vary a great deal, and many of them will not help you if you are complaining about a policy which their party supports. Quite a lot of them hold regular surgeries in the area they represent. You can get the name and address of your local councillor from the town hall.

● Local Ombudsman

If you are dissatisfied by a local council or a water authority, and you have already complained to them without success you may be able to get help from the local Ombudsman. The Ombudsman can help with:

● neglect and unjustified delay
● failure to follow agreed policies or rules
● malice, bias or unfair discrimination
● failure to have proper procedures

Write to the Local Ombudsman, 29 Castlegate, York YO1 1RN or 21 Queen Anne's Gate, London SW1H 9BU.

Age Allowance   *see* **Income Tax**

Aids and adaptations   *see* **Disabled**

Ante-natal care *see* **Babies**

Appeals

You have a right to appeal against most decisions taken by the **DHSS** about whether you are entitled to a benefit, and, if so, how much. Appeals against decisions taken by your local council about your **Housing Benefit** are dealt with under that heading. Appeals against medical decisions about **Mobility Allowance, Attendance Allowance** and **industrial benefits** are dealt with under those headings. There are no rights of appeal against most decisions about the **Social Fund.**

Decisions about **DHSS** benefits other than **Social Fund** payments are taken by an officer known as the adjudication officer. When a decision has been made you will either be sent a payment (usually with an explanation), or, if the decision is not to pay you, you will be sent a written decision with a notice telling you about your rights to appeal. There are some decisions you cannot appeal against. They are listed at the end of this article.

Delay

There is often a long delay between making your claim and getting a decision. You cannot officially appeal until you have been given a decision. Adjudication officers are supposed to make a decision within 14 days of being given the information they need. If you are sure that you have sent in all the necessary information and you haven't had a decision after 14 days then you could try appealing on the basis that no decision is effectively a decision not to pay you.

Time limits

You normally have three months from when you get your decision to appeal in. If you miss the time limit then you have a choice:

● you can ask the adjudication officer to review his or her decision. If they refuse to do this you have a fresh right to appeal against the refusal, or

● you can make a late appeal. Send it with an explanation of why it is late. It is up to the chairperson of the appeal tribunal to decide whether or not to accept it.

Reviews

Instead of an appeal you can ask for the adjudication officer's decision to be reviewed if you think it's wrong because:

● there's a mistake in the decision about what the law says
● there are facts the officer did not know or got wrong

You can ask for a review at any time. You should write a simple letter and explain your reasons. Keep a copy. A review can be much quicker than an appeal tribunal, particularly if there is some important fact which has been overlooked. If you have some document which is important for the decision send a copy with your letter.

If the **DHSS** agree to review their decision you should get arrears (*see* **Backdating**) from the date you requested a review.

Reasons

You have a right to a written statement of the reasons for any decision taken about you by an adjudication officer if you apply for it within 3 months of being given the written decision. You then have a right of appeal against the decision within 3 months of getting the statement of reasons.

If you appeal you will get a statement of reasons anyway, but it won't come until just before the appeal is heard. If your case is very complicated or difficult it might be helpful to ask for a statement before you appeal, because then you will be able to explain exactly why you think the adjudication officer is wrong. However this way will probably be a lot slower.

How to appeal

Appealing is simple. Write a letter to the local **DHSS** explaining exactly what decision you want to appeal against and what your reasons are. A copy of your appeal will be sent out with the papers to the members of the tribunal when the case is heard, so make your letter as clear and as full as you can. If you think you need advice, or more information, before you appeal you can write a simple one line letter saying that you want to appeal and that you will write and explain your reasons later.

What happens when you appeal?

You will get a letter from the appeal tribunal after about ten days which tells you that your appeal has been received and that you will be given a date for the hearing in due course. At the same time the staff in the **DHSS** will be looking again at their decision and considering the information in your appeal letter. Quite often they will reconsider their decision and award you your benefit without waiting for the appeal. Your appeal is then said to be 'superseded'. If that happens to you make sure that all the points you raised have been dealt with. If only part of your appeal is superseded you still have a right to a hearing.

Representatives

If you haven't had any advice before, now is the time to get some. Most of the organisations listed under **advice** will be able to find someone to represent you at a tribunal, even if they can't do so themselves. Your chances of success are much better if you go with a representative.

Although the tribunal is independent of the DHSS you are at a dis-advantage on your own because you don't know the rules.

Delay

You should be given at least ten days' notice of the hearing. If you aren't then the tribunal should only go ahead if you agree. You won't normally get a hearing until at least eight weeks after the date of your appeal, and in some places it may be much longer. If you think that the delay is unreasonable then you can write and complain to the clerk of the tribunal. The normal cause of the delay is that the **DHSS** hasn't prepared the papers. If you think that they have had a reasonable amount of time then you could write to the chairperson of the tribunal asking for the appeal to be listed even if the **DHSS** aren't ready.

Notice of the hearing

Together with the notice of the hearing you will get a detailed explana-tion of why the **DHSS** doesn't agree with you and a form from the tribunal to fill in. Fill in the form as soon as you can and send it back. You can use it to ask for the hearing to be held on a different day if you or your representative can't go on the day fixed. If your travelling expenses are more than £2 you can ask to be sent them in advance — otherwise you will get them on the day. You can get expenses for witnesses and for your representative (if they are not paid to represent you). You can claim for meals and loss of earnings. If you are not capable of going to the tribunal because you are too ill or disabled then you can ask for the tribunal to come to you.

Going alone

If you are not going to have a representative you will need to look at the section on **books**. This book does not try to deal with all the com-plications that may come up at an appeal. The best books to start with are the two CPAG handbooks. Using them you should be able to find the law which deals with your problem. The appeal papers, too, should tell you what the DHSS think the relevant law is.

Evidence

If the problem is really a dispute about facts, rather than about what the law means, then you should think about evidence which you can bring to the tribunal. You are allowed to bring documents, witnesses and even pictures to the hearing, if you think they will help to prove your case.

At the tribunal

Social security tribunals are usually quite informal. The chairperson, who is responsible for how the hearing is conducted, will be a lawyer, and there are two other members, who are also nothing to do with the **DHSS**. They sit on one side of the table, and you and your representative, if you have one, sit on the other side with the presenting officer from the **DHSS**. The clerk of the tribunal will be there, but takes no part in the decision.

Hearings are normally in public, but it is very unusual for any genuine members of the public to come. You can ask for a private hearing if you want to. If you want to you can go in and watch the case before yours, so that you have a better idea of what will happen.

It is up to the chairperson as to what happens at the hearing. Very often the **DHSS** will read out their papers first. You should have a chance to question the **DHSS** and point out anything you disagree with in the papers, and they will have a chance to question you.

The members of the tribunal will probably ask questions too. Make sure that you don't talk too fast. The chairperson will take notes and if you are too quick he may miss some of what you have to say.

Sometimes you, or the **DHSS**, or the tribunal will ask for an adjournment so that more evidence about something can be brought. It is up to the tribunal to decide whether to agree.

The decision

The tribunal will normally decide the appeal that day, and they may ask you if you would like to wait and hear the decision. In any case they will send you a full written decision about a week after the hearing from which you should be able to see how the decision was reached.

After the decision

If you win your appeal the **DHSS** should pay you about four weeks after the hearing unless they are considering appealing against the decision to the commissioner. They don't normally do that unless a lot of money is at stake. If you lose you can consider appealing to the commissioner. You have three months in which you can start your appeal.

Social security commissioners

The commissioners are judges who sit in London, Edinburgh, Cardiff and Belfast. Their job is to hear appeals against decisions made by tribunals. Their decisions are binding on tribunals, and the most important of them are published. You will probably see mentions of them in the tribunal papers. You can go and inspect the published decisions in your local **DHSS** office, or in main libraries. You will need **advice** if you are considering appealing to the commissioners.

No right of appeal

Some decisions are officially taken by the Secretary of State and you cannot appeal against them. They are mostly to do with **National Insurance** contributions, about how you must make your claim and how you are paid. Although you cannot **appeal** to a tribunal you may be able to go to court about these decisions, or you might be able to get help from your MP (*see* **Advice**).

How to find out more

Leaflet NI246 How to Appeal.

Appliances   *see* **Disabled**

Attachment of Earnings   *see* **Debts**

Attendance Allowance

Main conditions

You must be so severely disabled physically or mentally that you require attendance from another person which satisfies either the day condition or the night condition.

Day condition:

Either

a) 'frequent attention throughout the day in connection with his bodily functions'

or

b) 'continual supervision throughout the day in order to avoid substantial danger to himself or others'.

Night condition:
Either

a) 'prolonged or repeated attention throughout the night in connection with his bodily functions'

or

b) 'continual supervision throughout the night in order to avoid substantial danger to himself or others'.

Nightime supervision means 'to be awake for a prolonged period or frequent intervals for the purpose of watching over the claimant.'

What this means:
You should apply if you need help with any of these things:

- getting in or out of bed
- getting dressed or undressed
- using the toilet
- washing or shaving
- doing your hair
- taking a bath or shower
- going up or down stairs
- eating
- making a cup of tea

or if you need someone to be near you because any of these things apply to you:

- unsteady on your feet
- liable to fall or have an accident
- cannot pull yourself up in bed or out of a chair
- cannot see very well
- find it hard to make simple decisions
- don't really understand when something is dangerous
- cannot hear well enough to be able to manage
- cannot get up or down stairs safely

Amount
Higher rate £32.95 per week for day and night
Lower rate £22.00 per week for day or night

How paid
By order book. It will be combined with your **Income Support** order book if you have one. It can be paid by direct credit transfer to a bank account.

How to claim

Use the form on DHSS leaflet NI 205. Send it to the local office of the **DHSS**. A doctor will come to visit you and his report will be used to decide if you are entitled. You can apply for someone else if they can't do it themselves. Use the list above to check what to put on the form.

Age limits

Claimant must be over 2.

Children under 16 also have to show that they need supervision 'substantially in excess of that normally required by a child of the same age or sex'.

Excluded groups

People in hospital or local authority residential care for more than 28 days. Short periods will be added together if they are not separated by more than 28 days.

Time limits

You must have satisfied the conditions for at least six months before you are entitled. It is not possible to make a backdated claim at all, but an earlier claim for **Supplementary Benefit** or **Income Support** can be treated as a claim for Attendance Allowance if it should have been clear to the **DHSS** that you were entitled.

Taxable?

No.

Residence requirements

Must be in Great Britain and ordinarily resident here and have been here for at least 26 of the last 52 weeks.

Means tested

No.

Earnings rule

None.

Contribution test

None.

Effect on other benefits

Only counted as income for people on **Income Support** in residential care homes. Otherwise ignored.

May entitle the person caring for you to claim **Invalid Care Allowance**.

Effect of going into hospital

Attendance Allowance ceases after 28 days.

Effect of going abroad
Continues for first 26 weeks, and can continue for longer if you go for treatment.

Who administers it
DHSS Attendance Allowance Unit, Norcross, Blackpool, Tel: 0253 856123.

It often takes several months to process your claim, but if you get it you will get arrears paid back to the date you claimed.

Appeals
You cannot **appeal** against a refusal of Attendance Allowance. You can ask for a decision made by the Attendance Allowance Board to be reviewed. If you do this you will get a full explanation of why you have been turned down. You can appeal against an unsuccessful review to the social security commissioner. (*See* **Appeals**).

Special tips
Many people are turned down on their first application, but the success rate of people who ask for a review is very high. If there is anything at all tricky about your entitlement get **advice** as soon as you can — but claim straightaway, don't wait for the advice.

How to find out more:
Books: *Rights Guide to Non-Means-Tested Social Security Benefits, Disability Rights Handbook; DHSS Handbook on Non-Contributory Benefits.*

Leaflets: NI 205.

Organisations: Disability Alliance
Local DIAL Services
Hospital social workers

Available for work   *see* **Unemployed**

Babies

Benefits for pregnant women
The main benefit is now **Statutory Maternity Benefit** (SMP). To get it you must have been working for the same employer for at least six months ending with the 15th week before you expect to have your baby, that is the 25th week after conception. It should be easy to remember if you think

that you have to be in work the week after you conceive. You do not have to intend to go back to work after the baby is born to get the benefit.

If you cannot get SMP but you have paid **National Insurance** contributions of the right kind for at least 26 of the 52 weeks ending 14 weeks before the baby is due then you should qualify for **Maternity Allowance** from the **DHSS.**

If you are working you may also be entitled to maternity pay from your employer, depending on what it says in your terms of employment. You may also be entitled to return to work. Get booklet no. 4 *Employment Rights for the Expectant Mother* from the Jobcentre or Unemployment Benefit Office. You will be entitled to paid time off for ante-natal appointments. *See* **Employed** for more details.

Proof of pregnancy

For all maternity benefits you will need evidence to prove that you are pregnant. Your doctor or midwife should give you a maternity certificate (form Mat B1) when you are 26 weeks pregnant. You cannot be given it earlier and you cannot get a second copy. You can ask your doctor or midwife for an Expected Date of Confinement form but you might have to pay for it.

Health benefits

You can get free prescriptions and free dental treatment as soon as you are pregnant and for a year after the baby is born. Get form FW8 from your doctor or midwife as soon as you think you are pregnant.

If you are getting **Family Credit** or **Income Support** you can get free milk and vitamins while you are pregnant and until the baby is five years old. You can also get the cost of going to and from hospital for any reason, sometimes even if you are not getting any other benefit. *See* **Health Benefits** and **Hospital.**

Lump sum

A grant of £85 is paid through the **Social Fund** to women who qualify for **Family Credit** or **Income Support.** You can also claim the grant if you adopt a baby less than one year old. If a dependant child under 16 is pregnant then a person claiming **Income Support** or **Family Credit** for them can get the **Social Fund** payment. You can get the payment even if you go **abroad,** so long as you qualify.

Savings

For all **Social Fund** payments if your savings are more than £500 you will have to contribute the amount of the extra you have over £500. If you meet the conditions you are entitled to a payment, and you can **appeal** to the Social Security Appeal Tribunal if you are refused.

Delay in claiming

If you make a claim between three and twelve months after the date of the birth you will still be paid if you can show that there is good cause for your late claim. *See* **Backdating.** It does not matter whether you have bought the baby things before you make your claim.

How to apply

You must write to your local **DHSS** office when you are more than 29 weeks pregnant and ask them for a social fund application form. You must fill it in and return it to them with your maternity certificate (form Mat B1). You must apply before you have had the baby three months.

If you need more money

If you get **Income Support** you may be eligible for help from the **Social Fund.** *See also* DHSS leaflet FB8 Babies and Benefits, and NI17A Maternity Benefits.

Backdating

If you make a claim for a benefit which you have been entitled to for some time before you claimed it you may be able to get your claim backdated. There are different rules for different benefits. For many of them you have to show that you have a *Good Cause* for not having claimed before.

If you do not get a benefit (or not as much benefit as you should have) because of a mistake by the **DHSS** then you do not have to meet the same test. You should be able to claim back all the money you have lost because of official error. Sometimes you may be able to claim compensation, and interest on the money you have not had at the proper time.

Good cause for a late claim

If you don't claim a social security benefit within the time limit (the time limit is given for each benefit) you can usually get your claim backdated if you can show that there was *good cause* during the whole period before you claimed.

For most benefits you can only get 12 months' arrears, but for **Income Support, War Pensions** and Industrial Disablement Benefit there is no limit of this sort. *Good cause* does not apply to **Attendance Allowance** or **Mobility Allowance.**

The main reason why people don't claim what they are entitled to is, of course, that they don't know they are entitled. Ignorance on its own is not enough. You have to show that your ignorance was reasonable in the circumstances. So a mental handicap, or a severe physical illness will normally be a *good cause.*

If you are given bad, or insufficient, advice by someone on whom you could reasonably rely, such as a DHSS official, or a solicitor, that will normally be a *good cause.* If you make enquiries and misunderstand what you are told, that might be enough too. The person you ask must be a reliable source of information about benefits. If you ask your friends, or even your doctor, and they give you bad advice you will not succeed in your claim.

There are some occasions when the benefit you are entitled to is so obscure that you can show your ignorance is reasonable even though you do nothing to find out your rights — if a reasonable person would not have thought there were any rights to enquire about.

If you cannot read or write, or if you cannot speak good English, then you are at a disadvantage in finding out your rights, but you will need to demonstrate that you made some enquiries before you can show *good cause.* If there is any possibility that you are entitled to a benefit, you should make enquiries at your local **DHSS.** If you have done that unsuccessfully when you were in fact entitled then you may get your benefit backdated.

Backdated increases

If you are already getting a benefit but you think you should be paid at a higher rate then the rules are not quite the same. You are not asking for a new claim, but for a review of decisions made about a claim you have already made. You can usually ask for a review at any time, but you need to be able to point out some change of circumstances or a mistake, either about facts or about what the law says, which means that the original decision was wrong.

There is a rule which applies to most benefits that you cannot be paid arrears for more than a year because of a reviewed decision. This does not apply to decisions about **Income Support** if you can show that the decision was wrong because of some official error to which you did not contribute, or because you now have some evidence which you couldn't reasonably have produced at the time. You can also make an **appeal** out of time if you think you have a good case for a review but this rule would stop you getting paid.

If you find that you cannot be paid all the benefit you should have been paid because of these rules you can try claiming compensation from the **DHSS,** if you think it was their fault. It will probably help if you can get your MP involved. *See* **Advice.**

Bankrupt	*see* **Debts**
Bereaved	*see* **Death**
Bereavement Allowance	*see* **Widows**
Birth	*see* **Babies**

Blind

There are no special allowances for blind people. However you may get benefits because you are **disabled.** For example if you are blind you automatically qualify for an orange badge. Registered blind people get a premium to increase their entitlement to **Income Support** and **Housing Benefit,** and a blind child would automatically qualify for the disabled child premium (*see* **Disabled**). If you are blind you will not suffer deductions from your benefit for **non-dependants**.

The most valuable benefit for blind people is the RNIB, which is much the largest and richest charity for the disabled. Approach them if you need help. Address: Royal National Institute for the Blind, 224 Great Portland Street, London W1N 6AA.

A registered blind person is entitled to an extra tax allowance of £540 a year (1987/8).

There is a **DHSS** booklet in large print, FB19 Social Security Benefits: A guide for blind and partially sighted people.

Boarders

It is only for **Income Support** that it matters whether you are a boarder. For all other benefits it makes no difference whether you are a boarder or not. There are some special rules affecting **Attendance Allowance** if you are a boarder on **Income Support**.

Housing Benefit

If you are not on **Income Support** you can normally claim **Housing Benefit** as a boarder unless you are sponsored by the Council, or in their care. You would have to show how much of what you pay is rent, because you cannot get help from **Housing Benefit** for the cost of food, heating and so on.

Income Support

The rules about boarders on **Income Support** are very complicated. They have also changed a number of times in the last four years. If you have been a boarder at any time since 1984 you should get **advice** to make sure you haven't been underpaid. The Government is considering changing the rules again in April 1989.

If you are treated as a boarder your benefit will be made up of three parts: your personal allowance or pocket money, an amount for any meals not provided in your lodgings, and an amount for your board and lodging.

Who is a boarder?

You will be treated as a boarder if any of these apply:

- what you pay for your home includes the cost of any meals
- you live in a hotel, a guest-house, a hostel, bed and breakfast, a nursing home or a residential care home
- you are a refugee living in a refugee centre

but you will not be treated as a boarder if any of these apply:

- the person you board with is a close **relative**
- it is not a commercial arrangement
- you are on holiday and you have not been away from your normal home for 13 weeks
- the **DHSS** think you are working a fiddle
- you are between 16 and 19, and in care in a local authority establishment

Unemployed people under 25

If you are between 16 and 24, unemployed and signing on there are special restrictions. The Government say they are trying to prevent young unemployed people from leaving home to live in hotels at the seaside.

Most young people only get paid boarding allowance for a set time limit. After that they get paid a personal allowance only — £19.40 if under 18, £26.05 over 18 or £51.45 for a couple.

People who can escape from the time limits

You can continue to be treated as a boarder indenfinitely if any of these conditions apply to you or your **partner**

- you are over 25
- you don't have to sign on as **unemployed**
- you have a child
- you are pregnant
- you are physically or mentally **sick** or **disabled**
- you are in a hostel or you were placed in your lodgings as part of a scheme to help you back to a normal way of life

- you are on bail or under supervision from a probation officer or a social worker
- you are a **student** and you stay in the same lodgings in the holidays that you live in during term-time
- you are under 19 and have no parent or guardian, or you were forced to leave your family, or you are in care
- you are in the same lodgings you were in when you were in care or with foster parents
- you were in care less than twelve months ago
- you have been in the same lodgings for six months and you were not signing on before
- you are in the same accommodation as your parents

If none of these conditions apply to you you can still be treated as a boarder if you can persuade the **DHSS** that you would suffer exceptional hardship if they stopped paying you as a boarder.

What are the time limits?

If you are under 25 and not excused from the time limit, you cannot be paid as a boarder in bed and breakfast or lodgings in the same area for more than the time limit for that area. The time limits are generally two weeks anywhere south of Scotland near a seaside resort, four weeks for most of the country and eight weeks in London, Manchester, Birmingham and Glasgow. Once you have stayed for your set time you will not be paid as a boarder again in that area until six months have passed since you started being a boarder. You can move to another area and be a boarder there. The areas are quite large, so you might have to move quite a long way.

Cash limits

Even if you are treated as a boarder **DHSS** will only pay up to a fixed amount for full board. The amount you get depends on what sort of accommodation you live in and what area you are in. The cash limit does not apply for the first three months of your claim if you have lived in the same place for at least a year and you could afford to pay the charges when you moved in and you intend to move out.

For ordinary board and lodging the limit is £70 a week in London and between £45 and £60 in the rest of the country. This is to include all meals.

For hostels the limit is £70 a week everywhere.

For residential care homes the limit is between £130 and £190 a week depending on your health and age.

For nursing homes the limit is between £185 and £230 a week, depending on what sort of home it is. There is an extra £17.50 a week for homes in the London area.

Increasing the cash limit

So long as you don't get **Attendance Allowance,** you can get an addition of £17.50 a week to your cash limit in ordinary lodgings or a hostel if any of these apply:

● you are over pensionable age
● you have a **partner** and one of you is over 65
● someone you claim for is mentally or physically **disabled.**

You get the increase for each adult in the three categories above.

● you are pregnant or a mother with young children
● you are mentally ill and have been placed in a private household by a social worker

Cash limits for families

When you have worked out the cash limit that applies to you you can work out the limit for the family if you have one.

Each single adult or child over 11 gets the cash limit. A childless couple gets 1¾ times the cash limit A couple with any children under 11 gets twice the cash limit, plus an amount for each child. Each child under 11 gets £16.15 a week.

Meals out

The limits are to cover the cost of all your meals. If the charge you pay does not cover all your meals the cost of your full board will be worked out by adding on £1.10 for each breakfast and £1.55 for each lunch or dinner that you have to pay for.

Personal expenses

On top of this cash limit you get a pocket money allowance. In nursing homes and residential care this is £9.55 a week. In hostels and ordinary board and lodging the rates are given by this table:

	Basic rate	Higher rate
Single claimant	£10.30	£11.50
Couple	£20.60	£23.00
Dependant child over 18	£10.30	
16-17 years	£6.20	
11-15 years	£5.30	
Under 11 years	£3.45	

You qualify for the higher rate if you are entitled to any of the premiums for **Income Support** or if you have a child. If you are a boarder you don't actually get the premium.

What to do if you can't afford the charges

It may sound hard to believe, but the above is a very simplified version of the rules. You may be able to get extra help. And the rules may have changed by the time you read this.

If you are having problems, or if you think you will have problems in the future, get **advice** as soon as possible. You should get your name on the council housing list straight away. *See* **Homeless.** There is an organisation called CHAR, the Campaign for Housing and Single People, which has been campaigning on this issue. There may be a group in your area.

Books

Adviser. Bi-monthly magazine for advice workers. Covers social security, employment and housing. £7.50 a year from 63 Waterloo Road, Wolverhampton WV1 4QU.

Benefits. A housing and benefits guide for single people without a permanent home, CHAR.

Brown Books. Four large loose leaf volumes which contain The Law Relating to Social Security. You can look at them in your local **DHSS** office by appointment, or in large libraries.

CPAG's Benefits Guide for People Entering and Leaving the UK (Child Poverty Action Group).

CPAG's Housing Benefit Legislation, annotated and updated (CPAG).

CPAG's Non-Means-Tested Benefits: The Legislation. Bonner, Hooker, Smith and White: Sweet and Maxwell 1988, £19.50. The basic law, annotated in one volume, a companion to *Mesher.*

Disability Rights Handbook. Sally Robertson. 14th edition 1988 by Disability Alliance. £3.50. Very cheap and packed with information. Takes a wide view of disability and deals with many related subjects in a practical way.

Fuel Rights Handbook. 6th edition, SHAC/WRUG 1988, £5.95. Very thorough and comprehensive treatment of all problems relating to fuel.

Guide to Housing Benefit. McGurk and Raynsford, SHAC/Institute of Housing, 1988, £5.95.

Housing Benefits Guidance Manual. This is a large loose leaf volume published by **DHSS** containing their guidance to local authorities on how they should administer housing benefit. All CABx have a copy.

Housing Rights Guide, SHAC 1986, £4.95.

How to Cope with Credit and Deal with Debt, Ann Andrews and Peter

Houghton, Unwin, 1986, £2.95. This is a self-help guide with a kit of standard letters for readers to use.

Law relating to Housing Benefits. A loose leaf volume produced by the **DHSS**. Every CAB has a copy.

Mesher's CPAG's Means-Tested Benefits: The Legislation, John Mesher, £19.50. 5th edition 1988. Sweet and Maxwell. Contains not only the law but also detailed commentary on how it has been interpreted by the courts and the Commissioners. The advisers' bible.

National Welfare Benefits Handbook, Beth Lakhani and Jim Read. 18th edition 1988 by Child Poverty Action Group, £5.50. Very detailed clear and practical advice, written by advisers who know what they are talking about from first hand. The one book every claimant needs. Only £2.50 to individual claimants.

Neligan's Digest of Social Security Commissioner's Decisions. Two large loose leaf volumes which contain summaries of all the important Commissioner's decisions, indexed by subject. Very useful if you **appeal** because you may be able to find cases which support your argument. Available in your local **DHSS** office, by appointment, or in large libraries.

Ogus and Barendt's, The Law of Social Security. Second Edition, Butterworths, London, 1982. This is the standard legal textbook on the subject. It is very large and expensive and rather out-of-date, although there are supplements, but it contains a lot of information which is almost impossible to find elsewhere, particularly about older benefits like war pensions and National Insurance benefits.

Rights Guide to Non-Means-Tested Social Security Benefits, Jan Luba and Mark Rowland. 11th edition 1988 by Child Poverty Action Group, £4.50. A companion to the Handbook. The second book to buy. Only £2 to individual claimants.

Rights Guide for Homeowners, Lorraine Thompson and Jan Luba. 7th edition CPAG/SHAC, spring 1988, £3.50. A practical guide to keeping your home going.

Your Rights for Pensioners. 15th edition published in April 1988 by Age Concern England. About 80p.

Welfare Rights Bulletin. CPAG's twice monthly bulletin will keep you up-to-date. £7.50 for a year's subscription.

Budgetting loans	*see* **Social Fund**
Building Societies	*see* **Owner Occupiers**
Burial	*see* **Death**
Business	*see* **Self-employed**

Bus Passes

There is no national scheme to help either retired or **disabled** people with the cost of bus or train fares. It is up to your local council to run a scheme. If they do run a scheme it is up to them to decide how it runs and who is to benefit from it. If there is no scheme in your area go and see your local councillor and complain.

The Department of Transport produce an excellent guide full of information about transport for **disabled** people. You can get a copy from your local social services office or by writing to:

Department of Transport, Door-to-door Guide, FREEPOST, Victoria Road, South Ruislip, Middlesex HA4 0NZ.

You don't need a stamp.

Byssinosis	*see* **Industrial Benefits**

Capital

Means-tested benefits take your savings into account as well as your income.

The detailed rules for **Legal Aid** and **Health Benefits** are given under those headings, but they are based on the rules for **Family Credit, Income Support** and **Housing Benefit** which are given below. There are different rules for people who go into local authority residential accommodation: these are homes for old or disabled people. There is a good summary of the position in the *Disability Rights Handbook*, but the rules are not reproduced here because most of them are up to the discretion of the local authority.

The Capital rule for Income Support, Family Credit and Housing Benefit

All the savings that you and your **partner** own are added together. If the total is more than £6,000 you will not get any benefit. If your savings are between £3,000 and £6,000 you may get some benefit but it will be reduced by £1 per week for each £250 you have over £3,000. This is called tarriff income and has no relation to the income you actually get from your savings.

If your child has capital of more than £3,000 you may still get benefit but it will not include any dependant allowance for the child. Apart from this your child's capital does not affect your claim.

Your home

The value of your home is completely ignored if you normally live in it. So is money deposited with a housing association. If you have sold your home within the past six months and are planning to buy a new home with that money it will be ignored for as long as the **DHSS** think reasonable. Similarly, if you have bought a home and not yet moved in the value will be ignored for six months or as long as the **DHSS** think reasonable. If you have money given or borrowed for repairs, replacements or improvements it is normally ignored for six months, or longer. *See also* **Owner Occupiers.**

Valuation of your belongings

Your investments will be valued for what you could sell them for, apart from current National Savings Certificates, which are valued at cost. Your personal possessions are not counted unless you acquired them in order to claim benefit.

If it will cost you something to turn property into cash there will be a deduction of 10% for the cost of the sale. If there is a debt or charge like a mortgage secured on your property then the value of the charge will be deducted. Apart from that there is no provision for counting your debts against your assets. If you have liabilities then you must pay them, or part of them, if your assets are worth more than £6,000, otherwise you will not get any benefit.

If you have any life assurance or endowment policies their surrender value is ignored. Any premises occupied by an elderly or incapacitated relative or by your former **partner** are disregarded.

Arrears paid to you of **Attendance** or **Mobility Allowance** will be ignored for up to a year after you have received the payment.

Any business assets you own can be ignored if it seems reasonable to the **DHSS** to do so. They are more likely to ignore the assets of a business which may take you off benefit than one which is going downhill.

Money held in trust which you are entitled to is counted as yours, unless it is money for a personal injury (in which case it is ignored for at least two years) or a discretionary trust.

Notional resources

You can sometimes be treated as having resources which you don't actually possess. This can happen:

- if there is some money which is available to you if you apply for it
- if you deliberately get rid of your capital (or income) in order to claim **Income Support** or **Housing Benefit.** The law in this area is confusing. If you think this may happen to you you should get **advice.**
- if money is paid to someone else on behalf of a member of your family which is either derived from social security or used for the food, clothing or housing of that person.

If you are refused benefit because of your capital you may still be able to claim. *See* **Emergencies.**

## Carer	*see* **Disabled**
## Caring for a sick person	*see* **Disabled** **Invalid Care Allowance**
## Cars	*see* **Mobility Allowance**
## Central heating	*see* **Fuel**
## Channel Islands	*see* **Abroad**
## Charitable payments	*see* **Income**

Child Benefit

Main conditions

You must be responsible for a child. The child need not be related to you. If the child does not live with you you must pay at least £7.25 a week for its maintenance. People who are under 19 and in full-time non-advanced education count as children. *See* **Students.**

Amount

£7.25 per week.

How paid

Order book or direct transfer to bank account. Paid four-weekly in arrears unless that would cause hardship.

How to claim
Form CB 2 and 3 from your local **DHSS.**

Age limits
None for claimants. Child must be under 19.

Excluded groups
Married children. Children who are in prison or in care for more than 8 weeks.

Time limits
You can only claim one year's backpay.

Taxable
No.

Residence requirements
Child and claimant must be in Great Britain. Temporary absence, normally not more than 8 weeks, but up to 3 years for boarding education, does not affect benefit. Claimant and either child or a parent must have been in Great Britain for more than six months in the last year.

Means tested
No.

Contribution test
None.

Effect on other benefits
Children who get **Severe Disablement Allowance** cannot get Child Benefit. It is taken into account for **Income Support** and **Housing Benefit** but ignored for **Family Credit.**

Effect of going abroad
Benefit continues for first eight weeks of a temporary absence.

Special tips
You can still get benefit for a child under 19 who is doing non-advanced further education (this means up to A-level standard), and to the end of December if your child leaves school in the summer and has not started a **Youth Training Scheme** place. For children who leave school at other times you keep your Child Benefit for three months if your child has neither a job nor a YTS place. If your child registers for a YTS place but one isn't available straightaway they get a YTS Bridging Allowance.

You need to write to the Child Benefit Centre to let them know what your children are doing. *See* **Students** for more details.

Who administers it
Child Benefit Centre, PO Box 1, Newcastle upon Tyne, NE88 1AA. Tel. 091 416 6722.

Appeals
If you are refused benefit you can **appeal** to a Social Security Appeal Tribunal.

How to find out more
Books: *Rights Guide to Non-Means-Tested Benefits*

DHSS Leaflets:
CH 1   Child Benefit
CH 4   Child Benefit for children away from home
CH 4a Child Benefit for children in the care of the local authority
CH 5   Child Benefit for people entering Britain
CH 6   Child Benefit for people leaving Britain
CH 7   Child Benefit for children aged 16 and over

Childminding

Childminding is one of a very few ways in which a person on **Income Support** can make themselves better off legally. Even if you work for more than 24 hours a week you will still be able to claim **Income Support** if you work as a childminder at home.

If you claim **Housing Benefit** or **Family Credit** you should be treated as **self-employed.** This means that you can deduct your expenses from the money you receive to work out your profit. Only one third of that will count as income, and it will be assessed after tax etc and then £5 (or £15) a week of that will be ignored.

If you are an approved childminder then you can get one third of a pint of milk a day free from Social Services for each child.

Children

The basic, universal, benefit for children is **Child Benefit.** This replaces the old tax allowances for children.

If you are a **single parent** you are also entitled to **One Parent Benefit.** A **widow** with a child under 19 is entitled to **Widowed Mother's Allowance.** If you are looking after a child who is effectively an orphan you may get **Guardian's Allowance.**

If you are working more than 24 hours a week you may be entitled to **Family Credit.** If you have rent or rates to pay you may be entitled to **Housing Benefit** on top of any other benefits you might get.

Most children will be entitled to free **legal aid** in their own right, and to free **health benefits** and **hospital** fares. If you have children you may be entitled to these benefits and to **Income Support** too, if your income is low.

Increases in benefits for children

With many Social Security benefits you can claim an increase for children. You cannot claim anything for your children on **Unemployment Benefit, Sickness Benefit** (unless you are over pensionable age), **Statutory Maternity Pay, Maternity Allowance,** or **Statutory Sick Pay.** If you have children you will probably have to claim **Income Support** as well as the other benefit.

You can get an increase for children with:

- **Retirement Pension**
- **Widowed Mother's Allowance**
- **Invalidity Benefit**
- **Invalid Care Allowance**
- **Severe Disablement Allowance**

The additional amount is £8.40 a week for each child. For the details *see* **Dependants.**

See **Hospital** for how your benefits are affected if you or your child goes into hospital.

Children and Income Support

Income Support is paid to families, and the needs of children living with you are included in the calculation of what you need to live on. It makes no difference whether the children are related to you. The amounts for children are not generous. You get £1.54 a day for a child under 11.

If a child is in possession of more than £3,000 **capital,** then their needs will not be taken into account in your assessment, although you will still get the *family premium* and the *lone parent premium* in respect of them.

You can continue to claim **Income Support** for a child who has left school but not yet got a **Youth Training Scheme** place as long as they get **Child Benefit**. The rules about when children can claim **Income Support** for themselves are given under **Students.**

You will not get **Income Support** for a child who is:

- **abroad** for more than 4 weeks
- in possession of an **income** higher than the benefit you would claim for him
- in prison or a similar institution or in care and living away from you
- officially fostered by you
- in **hospital** or a home for more than 12 weeks and you do not visit or stay in touch
- about to be adopted by you

You should be able to get benefit for a child who comes to stay with you temporarily, even if they are normally in an institution.

Children and the Social Fund

You can get a Community Care Grant from the **Social Fund** to ease exceptional pressure on you and your family. If you have a **disabled** child you are a high priority for help. You can also qualify for **travelling expenses** for your children or for someone to look after them if there is a domestic crisis, or for the cost of visiting your child if it is in the care of your former **partner** and custody has not yet been decided by the Court.

Children, Family Credit and Housing Benefit

The rules for children and these benefits are similar to those for **Income Support.** If a child has **income** or **capital** then it affects your benefit only as far as the amount of extra benefit you would have got for the child.

How to find out more

If you are having trouble with your children, with either money or other things, your local Social Services office is probably the best place to get help.

For details of when and how children can claim benefits in their own right *see* **Students.**

See also **DHSS** leaflets FB27 Bringing up Children, and FB23 Young People's Guide to Social Security.

Christmas Bonus

If you are getting one of the benefits listed below in a week just before Christmas (usually the first week in December) you qualify for an extra bonus payment of £10. It is added to your order book for that week automatically if you have an order book; otherwise it is sent to you as a giro. If you don't get it when you think you should, contact your local **DHSS** office.

The benefits which qualify you for it are:

- **Retirement Pension**
- Widow's Benefit
- **Attendance Allowance**
- **Invalid Care Allowance**
- **Invalidity Benefit**
- **Severe Disablement Allowance**
- **Income Support** if you are over 60, **sick** or **disabled**
- Constant Attendance Allowance
- Unemployability Supplement
- War Disablement Pension if you have retired
- War Widow's Pension

It is not counted as **income** for **means-tested** benefits.

Leaflet: NI 229

Citizens' Advice Bureau
see **Advice**

Civil Legal Aid
see **Legal Aid**

Claims
see **Backdating**
DHSS

Cleaning
see **Transitional Protection**

Close Relatives	*see* **Relatives**
Coastguard	*see* **Income**
Cohabiting	*see* **Partner**
College	*see* **Students**
Commissioners	*see* **Appeals**
Community Care Grants	*see* **Social Fund**
Community Charge	*see* **Rates**

Community Programme

The Community Programme is the Government's main scheme for creating jobs. It is run by the Manpower Services Commission (MSC). In many areas it is the only way an **unemployed** person is likely to find work.

Proposed changes

In September 1988 there will be major changes. The MSC will be re-named the Training Commission and the new Community Programme will become part of the wider training scheme. Payments will be based on the benefit you were getting while unemployed, together with a premium. It is expected that people over 50 will not be encouraged to apply. Participants will probably not be employees,. *See* **Job Training Scheme** for more details of what is proposed.

Who is eligible for the Community Programme?

You must have been continuously unemployed for the last twelve months and drawing benefit at the time you are offered the job. In some circumstances you may still be eligible if your **partner** is drawing benefit for you. Priority is given to people under 50 who have been unemployed for more than two years.

What do you get?

You are employed by a project, not by the MSC. You will usually be taken on for a year, or for the length of the project, if that is less. If your employer wants to keep you on for another year s/he will have to show that there are no unemployed people available who could do your job. Most of the jobs are part-time, and you can't normally work overtime or get overtime pay.

Effect on other benefits

You are treated as **employed,** so you will have to pay **National Insurance** Contributions if you earn more than £41 a week. Because the wages are so low you may still be entitled to other benefits. *See* **Employed.**

You may be entitled to **Statutory Sick Pay** if you are ill, or **Statutory Maternity Pay** if you are pregnant.

Company pension   *see* **Retired**

Compensation

If you or your belongings are damaged either deliberately or accidentally you may be able to get compensation from the person who was responsible.

To make a claim you must show that the person who caused the damage was negligent towards you. That means that s/he should have taken care to see you were not injured and s/he didn't. A person can only be negligent if s/he could have seen that harm might come from what s/he did. So if your employers have a dangerous machine and don't put a guard around it they may be found negligent if you are damaged by it. It may also be a criminal offence for them to have an unguarded machine.

A person can only be negligent if s/he could tell that you might be damaged by his/her action (or lack of action). So if your landlord does not know that your bedsitter needs repairing you will not be able to get compensation from him if you or your belongings are damaged by it. It is important, for this reason, that you not only tell your landlord (or whoever it may be) what the problem is but also that you tell them in writing and keep a copy, so that you can prove that you did tell them.

To make a claim you will probably need a solicitor if your problem is at all serious, and you should choose one who is experienced in this sort of work. You must normally claim within three years of the event which caused your injury.

If you are injured by a violent crime or in trying to stop or catch a criminal *see* **Criminal Injuries Compensation.** *See* **Disabled** for details of other benefits which are available to all disabled people. *See* **Industrial Benefits** if you are injured at work. *See* **Capital** for the affect your compensation money could have on your benefits.

Constant Attendance Allowance *see* Industrial Benefits

Contracted out *see* National Insurance

Contributions *see* National Insurance

Cooking charge *see* Housing Benefit

Council housing *see* Housing Benefit

Councillors *see* Advice

Couples *see* Partner

Covenants *see* Students

Credits *see* National Insurance

Criminal Injuries Compensation

This is a special scheme for people who are seriously injured because of a crime of violence or while attempting to catch a criminal. There are separate ways of getting **compensation** if your property is damaged or your injuries are not serious enough for this scheme.

Main conditions
You must be seriously injured, either in a crime of violence, or in trying to catch a criminal or prevent a crime.

Amount
You normally get a lump sum. The amount depends on how badly you were injured and what effect your injury has on you.

How paid
Normally to the person who was injured. If they have died their dependants may be paid both compensation for the death and also the cost of the funeral.

How to claim
Get a form from the Criminal Injuries Compensation Board.

Age limits
None.

Excluded groups
There are special rules if you and the attacker were living together at

the time of the injuries. You cannot claim if you were injured in a road accident unless the injury was caused deliberately. If you contributed to the attack, or if you have a bad criminal record, you may not get an award.

Time limits
You should claim as soon as possible, even if your attacker is unknown or not yet arrested.

Taxable
No.

Residence requirements
The injury must have happened in Great Britain.

Means tested
No.

Earnings rule
The compensation you get may be affected by the earnings you lose because of the injury.

Effects on other benefits
Any benefits you get because of the injury will be taken off the award of compensation.

Who administers it
Criminal Injuries Compensation Board, Whittington House, 19 Alfred Place, London, WC1E 7LG.

Special tips
You must co-operate with the police and the Board by reporting the crime at once and giving them information.

Appeals
If you are not satisfied with a decision you are entitled to a hearing by three members of the Board.

How to find out more
Books: *Disability Rights Handbook*

Leaflets: The Board publish a leaflet called 'Victims of Crimes of Violence', which you can get free from them or from a Citizens' Advice Bureau.

Organisations: A solicitor would be the best source of advice.

Criminal Legal Aid
see **Legal Aid**

Crisis Loans	*see* **Emergencies**
Custody	*see* **Prisoners**
Damages	*see* **Compensation**
Deafness	*see* **Disabled**

Death

The old £30 Death Grant was abolished on 6 April 1987. It has been replaced by help through the **Social Fund,** which will be available to anyone on **Income Support, Housing Benefit** or **Family Credit** who is responsible for a funeral. You do not have to be related to, or even know, the dead person, so long as you have paid, or intend to pay the bill.

How to claim
There are claim forms with notes available for funeral payments at **DHSS** offices. You must claim within three months of the date of the funeral.

What you get
You get the cost of what the **DHSS** consider to be the reasonable cost of a funeral. This includes

- documents, such as a death certificate
- a coffin
- transport of the coffin and bearers and one other car
- undertaker's fees and gratuities
- chaplain's, organist's, cemetery or cremation fees for a simple funeral
- religious expenses up to £75
- bringing the body home within the UK, if necessary
- one return journey for arranging the funeral

If your savings are more than £500 you will have to contribute the amount of the extra you have over £500. If you meet the conditions you are entitled to a payment, and you can **appeal** to the Social Security Appeal Tribunal if you are refused.

Delay in claiming
If you make a claim between three and twelve months after the date of the death you will still be paid if you can show that there is good cause for your late claim. See **Backdating.** It does not matter whether you have paid for the funeral before you make your claim.

Reclaiming the money

Any money which the dead person left which is available to you without probate or letters of administration being granted will be deducted from the payment. So will any money from a life insurance policy. If a relative or charity pays for any special funeral arrangement not covered by the **DHSS** that will be ignored. Otherwise any payments from relatives or charities will be taken off your payment.

If the dead person leaves any money the **DHSS** will reclaim the payment from the estate, but not from a house left to a **partner** or from the value of personal possessions left to relatives.

Fares to the funeral

If you are not arranging the funeral, you can claim the cost of fares within the UK to the funeral or cremation of a close **relative** from the **Social Fund.**

Sorting things out

If the dead person left any money then the cost of the funeral is the first charge on the estate. If there is not enough money to pay the dead person's debts, relatives do not have to pay. If the dead person was getting any benefit then the giros or order book will have to be sent back. If there is no one to arrange or pay for the funeral then the Council will pay for a very basic funeral.

The Inland Revenue produce a leaflet for the person sorting out the estate: IR 45 What happens when someone dies.

If the dead person was getting **Income Support** the **DHSS** will check the probate register to make sure that they didn't have too much **capital** to get benefit. If they did then the executors will be asked to pay it back. *See* **Overpayments.**

If they were getting **Family Credit** then another adult (normally the **partner**) may be appointed to receive the rest of the payments which are due.

If they were getting **Housing Benefit** then you should notify the Council of the death.

If your husband has died then see **Widow's Payment.** If your wife has died then you may be able to use her **National Insurance** Contributions to improve your **Retirement Pension.**

If your **partner** has died and you have children *see* **Single Parents.**

If the person died through war injuries *see* **War Pensions.** If they died because of an industrial injury or disease *see* **Industrial Benefits.** If they died as a result of violent crime, or trying to stop a crime, then *see* **Criminal Injuries Compensation.** If you think someone was to blame for the death then *see* **Compensation.**

How to find out more

The **DHSS** produce an excellent leaflet: D 49 What To Do After a Death. It is very practical and deals with the problems of funerals and wills as well as benefits. FB 29 Help when Someone Dies gives more details about benefits.

Organisations which will help:

Age Concern deal with all sorts of problems which affect the over 60s. Look in the phone book for your local branch.

The Compassionate Friends is a self-help group for bereaved parents. Contact them at 50 Woodwaye, Watford, Herts WD1 4NW

The Foundation for the Study of Infant Deaths, 5th floor, 4 Grosvenor Place, London SW1X 7HD

The Stillbirth Association, 15a Christchurch Hill, London NW3 1JY

Debts

If you owe more than you can pay do not borrow more money to pay off your creditors. Usually you end up losing even more that way. If you cannot pay you should tell your creditors so. You cannot be imprisoned for debt any more. The worst that can happen is:

- Distraint on goods. This means bailiffs come and take your furniture and belongings to sell. It is very rare for bailiffs actually to remove your belongings, because most second-hand goods are not worth enough to pay for the expenses of the sale.
- A garnishee order. Your bank account is emptied and paid over to your creditors.
- Attachment of earnings. Money is stopped out of your pay by your employer and paid to your creditors.
-
- Administration order. If you have at least one court order and your debts are less than £5,000 in total you can ask the court to make this order. The court will order you to pay something to the court regularly and this will be shared among your creditors. None of them can take any further action.
- Bankruptcy. The Official Receiver will take over all your affairs and sell your belongings to pay your debts. You are allowed to keep certain personal possessions, and usually the Receiver would not want to sell your personal belongings unless they were valuable.

While you are bankrupt you cannot borrow money without telling the person you are borrowing from that you are bankrupt. You are also not allowed to stand for Parliament, or be elected to a local council, or hold various other public offices.

If you have not been bankrupt before and you have not committed fraud, then after three years you will be automatically discharged, even if you have still not paid your debts.

If you have a lot of debts which you are not going to be able to pay it is worth considering going bankrupt or getting an Administration Order. You get the forms you need for either from your nearest County Court. If your debts are more than you can manage then get **advice** as soon as possible.

For details of when the **DHSS** might lend you money, or make you a grant, *see* **Social Fund.**

Deductions from benefit   *see* **Fuel Overpayments**

Deductions from pay   *see* **Debts Employed**

Delay   *see* **Advice DHSS**

Delay in claiming   *see* **Backdating**

Dental Treatment   *see* **Health Benefits**

Dependants

With many Social Security benefits you can claim an increase for your wife, your husband or your **children.** The amounts, and whether you can claim, are listed under each benefit. These are the general rules which apply to all benefits listed below. The rules for **student grants** and **War Pensions** are not listed here because they are quite different.

Children
You cannot claim any addition for your children to **Unemployment Benefit, Sickness Benefit, Statutory Maternity Pay,** or **Statutory Sick Pay.**

Children and means-tested benefits

If you claim **Income Support, Housing Benefit, Family Credit** or **Legal Aid** your benefit will be assessed including the needs of any **children** in your household. For these benefits a child is a person under 16 or under 18 if still at school or college. See **students** for the rules on when **children** can claim in their own right if they are at college.

If your child spends only part of a week with you and part with someone else it will be treated as part of the family of the person who claims **Child Benefit.** If neither of you does then it will be treated as part of the family of the person who has primary responsibility.

Children and National Insurance benefits

You can get an increase for **children** if you claim:

- **Retirement Pension**
- **Widowed Mother's Allowance**
- **Invalidity Benefit**
- **Invalid Care Allowance**
- **Severe Disablement Allowance**

The amount is £8.40 a week for each child.

To get the increase for a child you or your **partner** must get **Child Benefit** for the child and if the child doesn't live with you you must pay at least that amount for the child's maintenance.

If you have a **partner** you don't get the increase for your children if your partner earns more than £90 a week. This earnings rule is increased to £95 for a second child and by £10 for each extra child. *See* **Income** for how to work out the amount.

See also **Children.**

Wives and husbands

You can claim an increase of most benefits for a wife or husband. The amounts are different for the various benefits. The rules for means-tested benefits are different, and in particular don't distinguish between married and unmarried people. *See* **Partner** for more details.

You have to show:

- that you are legally married
- that either you live together or you pay maintenance of at least as much as the increase in the benefit
- that he or she is not earning more than the amount of the increase

The rules for **Retirement Pension** are more complicated. See that heading.

Dependants looking after children

This is how you can claim an increase of a contributory benefit for a **partner** if you are not married, but it can apply also to people of the same sex and even to people who do not live together at all. You could get this increase if you lived with your wife or husband who was working and some other person was looking after your child. You could not get the increase if the dependant was not in Great Britain.

To get this increase you have to show that:

● you aren't getting an increase for a wife or husband
● your dependant is looking after a child for whom you get **Child Benefit** and the child increase mentioned above
● either you live together
or you pay your dependant at least the amount of the increase in maintenance
or you employ them and pay them at least the amount of the increase
● apart from what you pay them they don't earn more than the amount of the increase. There is a higher earnings limit for some benefits of £31.45 a week.

You can only get one increase for an adult dependant, no matter how many dependants or children you may have.

See also **Non-dependants.**

Deposit
see **Social Fund**

Designated course
see **Student grant**

The DHSS

The DHSS is a large and complicated organisation. To get the best out of it you need to know a bit about how it works — if it works. In some cities, and especially in inner London, the DHSS offices have been in a state of near collapse for several years and the enormous changes in April 1988 will probably have finished them off. In those offices you may have difficulty getting a response of any kind.

Central offices

Some benefits are dealt with centrally, in the big offices in Blackpool and Newcastle. The address and telephone number is given by each benefit. These offices can be very slow to respond to letters and impossible to get through to on the telephone, especially if your problem is one which affects large numbers of people at the same time, such as **Child Benefit** for school leavers in September. If the matter is urgent you could try ringing very early in the morning — 8 a.m. or earlier. The staff work flexitime and you are more likely to catch them then (unless my advice proves popular).

Local offices

Most benefits are dealt with in integrated local offices, which cover a local area. Although they are called integrated they actually contain two quite separate parts.

The contributory side deals with the respectable benefits — **Retirement, Invalidity** and **Widows.** The staff are fairly relaxed. They usually know the rules because they have barely changed over the last 40 years. The staff stay in their jobs long enough to know what they are doing, and they will give you advice and help. You can often make an appointment to go in and see someone by name. You might even get a cup of tea in some of the quiet rural offices.

The other side deals with **Income Support** — the new Poor Law. You will be able to see which side is which without looking for notices. On the **Income Support** side all the chairs are screwed to the floor. There is usually a thick partition of armoured glass between you and the receptionist. People queue to shout at the clerk behind the glass through the little slit at the bottom. Everyone in the waiting room can hear all the intimate details. Some people get very upset and angry. That's why the chairs are screwed down. Because of the pressure the staff often don't stay long, especially in London. They often don't know what the rules are, partly because they haven't the time to find out, and partly because the Government keeps changing them.

Changing the rules

Changing the rules (or moving the goalposts during the game) seems to be part of the Government's strategy to make sure people don't claim what they are entitled to. Since 1979 there has not been a year without major change to some part of the social security system, and some years there have been three or four. In general very little publicity is given either to changes in benefits or to encourage the take-up of benefits. Even the

Government admits that some benefits are claimed by less than half of those who should get them.

Dealing with local offices

If you ring up tell the switchboard operator your surname and the benefit you are claiming. The switchboard usually opens at 8.30 am, before the doors open at 9.30 am. You will normally speak to a clerk. Although clerks make most routine decisions they are not responsible for them. If you think a decision is wrong, or your problem is complicated, ask to speak to the supervisor. A supervisor is responsible for a section. On the contributory side a section may deal with one or more benefits for the whole office. On the **Income Support** side the normal rule is for a section to be responsible for a part of the alphabet, with some special sections dealing with particular issues, like fuel direct, or fraud, for the whole alphabet. Sometimes **Income Support** for pensioners is dealt with separately.

Although a telephone call can be useful as a way of finding out what, if any, decision has been made about you, a letter is a much better way for you to communicate important information. Telephone messages are often not recorded, and if they are noted down they can easily be lost. If you write, you can keep a copy to produce if no action results. You should always keep anything they send to you. If things go wrong you, or an adviser, might be able to tell what is the matter from reading the DHSS papers.

Lost papers

If you are told that your papers cannot be found do not worry too much. The way the office is organised means that if anyone, anywhere in the office, needs to take any action on your case — such as sending out your giro — your papers will not be available for anyone else. If your papers have not been found after a week, ask to speak to the supervisor, who can arrange a more thorough search.

Fares to the office

The DHSS can pay the cost of your fares to the local office over and above 80p a week if they call you in or if it is cheaper or more satisfactory for you to come in than to write or telephone. They won't pay unless you ask, and even if you ask they aren't forced to pay.

Lost giros

Once it has been decided that you are entitled to a benefit the DHSS are obliged to pay you. You are not paid until you actually receive your giro or order book. If your giro doesn't arrive for any reason you must report it missing straight away. You should ask for an immediate replacement. In many offices you will be told that you will have to wait for up to three months to see if your giro turns up. If you cannot afford to wait so long you should get **advice** from a solicitor. You can threaten to sue the Secretary of State for Social Services for not paying you the money you are owed. In practice if you can convince the local DHSS that you are serious they will replace your giro straight away. You can get a useful booklet called *Lost Giros — how to replace them,* from Merseyside Welfare Rights Resource Centre, 24 Hardman Street, Liverpool L1.

No joy?

If you are not getting anywhere then *see* **Advice** or **Appeals.** You can normally only appeal if you have had a decision. If the problem is that you are waiting for a decision then *see* **Advice.** Look at the section on Members of Parliament. They are often the best way of getting your case looked at quickly.

Diabetes   *see* **Disabled**

Direct Payments   *see* **Fuel**
                                                    Income Support

Disabled

This section deals with benefits for people whose disability is likely to be permanent. In practice this means lasting more than six months with no immediate prospect of getting better. If you think you are likely to get better fairly soon then *see* **Sick.**

How you became **disabled** makes a great deal of difference to the benefits you get. This table shows the different benefits which are affected. The best benefits are at the top. They are better because they give you more money, they are easier to qualify for, and you are less likely to lose them if your circumstances change.

How you became disabled	Benefits you can claim
Injured in war or the Forces	War Pensions
Injured at work or through an industrial disease	Industrial Benefits
Accident	Compensation
Any cause after you had started your working life and paid National Insurance Contributions	Invalidity Benefit Sickness Benefit Statutory Sick Pay

As a result of vaccination   **Vaccine Damage Payment**

At birth or before you had   **Severe Disablement**
paid enough **National Insurance**   **Allowance**
Contributions

There are other benefits which you may be entitled to regardless of how you became disabled, depending on what your disability is and what your circumstances are.

Benefits for specific disability

Mobility Allowance   for people who are unable, or almost unable, to walk.

Attendance Allowance   for people who need a lot of looking after because they are physically or mentally disabled.

Invalid Care Allowance   for a person who looks after someone who gets **Attendance Allowance.**

Income Support   if you are assessed as a disabled person you get an extra premium.

Family Fund   for a family with a severely disabled child.

Social Fund   you may be able to get a grant or loan, and your chances are much improved if you need help because you or a member of your family are disabled.

Practical help for disabled people

This book does not deal with practical help for disabled people apart from the financial side of things. If you need any sort of practical help because of your disability contact either your doctor or your Social Services office.

Your home and your disability

You may be able to get help to adapt your home, for example, to put in handrails or an extra toilet. *See* **Owner Occupiers.**

If you have some special facility in your home which you need because of your disability, whether or not it was put in specially, then you should not have to pay **rates** on it. *See* **Disabled Rate Relief.** You should be able to get this relief even if you don't pay the rates yourself.

Transport for disabled people

If you cannot walk, or your walking is very limited, you may be able to get an Orange Badge and/or exemption from road tax. You can get these even if you cannot get **Mobility Allowance** because, for example, you are too old. See your Social Services office for an application form.

The Department of Transport produce an excellent guide full of information about transport for disabled people. You can get a copy from your local Social Services office or by writing to:

Department of Transport, Door-to-door Guide, FREEPOST, Victoria Road, South Ruislip, Middlesex HA4 0NZ. You don't need a stamp.

How your disability affects means-tested benefits

For **Housing Benefit** and **Income Support** your benefit will be assessed using an additional premium if you are disabled.

You qualify for the ordinary Disability Premium (£13.05 for a single person, £18.60 for a couple) if you or your **partner** get **Attendance Allowance, Mobility Allowance** (or its equivalent), **Invalidity Pension** or **Severe Disablement Allowance,** or are registered **blind,** or the claimant is treated as having been incapable of work for at least 28 weeks.

You qualify for the Severe Disability Premium (£24.75 for each person qualifying) if you get **Attendance Allowance** but have no-one getting **Invalid Care Allowance** for you, and you have no **non-dependants** living with you. If you do have a non-dependant living with you you can keep the higher premium if the non-dependant gets **Attendance Allowance** too, or if they are a **boarder,** or a carer supplied by a charity.

If you have a disabled child you qualify for a Disabled Child Premium (£6.15) if the child gets **Attendance Allowance** or **Mobility Allowance,** or is registered **blind,** so long as they do not have more than £3,000 capital.

Normally, if you are working more than 24 hours a week you cannot get **Income Support,** no matter how poor you are. But if your earning power is reduced by at least 25% because of your disability you can.

Disabled students

If you are disabled you are probably more likely to get a discretionary student grant from your local authority, particularly for courses you can study at home such as Open University courses.

If you get a mandatory **Student Grant** you can get an extra amount of up to £555 (1986/7) for the cost of any extra expense caused by your disability. This might be for equipment you need, like a typewriter, or to pay a helper. You can also get the cost of extra travel. If you get a discretionary grant you might also get either of these extra allowances.

There are also special provisions for disabled **students** to claim **Income Support.** If you do not have to sign on to get your benefit you can do any course you like without your **Income Support** being affected. The only thing you would need to watch is that if your studies are successful the **DHSS** may say that you are capable of working and stop any benefits you get because you are not capable of working.

Health Benefits
Disabled children who are between 5 and 16 and not at school can get free milk. With some long-term medical problems you get free prescriptions. *See* **Health Benefits.** You may be able to get the cost paid of any trips you make to hospital. *See* **Hospital.**

Registering as disabled
The Social Services Department keeps a register of disabled people. Being on the register doesn't mean that you are entitled to anything you couldn't get without registering, but it does mean that you have some official proof of your disability if you ever need it. It may also help you, indirectly, if the Social Services Department has a proper record of the number of disabled people in their area so they can plan their policies.

A quite separate register of disabled people is kept by the Manpower Services Commission at the Jobcentre. If you are on their register you will be given a green card. Firms which employ more than 20 people are supposed to employ at least 3% disabled people. Unfortunately this law is never enforced, so you are very unlikely to get a job through the quota.

Finding work
If you are registered with the MSC there are a number of services designed to help you train and find work. You should go and see the Disablement Resettlement Officer at the Jobcentre if you are interested in any of them. These services are:

- Job Introduction scheme: The MSC will pay a firm £45 a week for six weeks to take a disabled person on trial.

- Aids and adaptations: MSC will lend special tools or make grants of up to £6,000 for adapting buildings.

- Fares to work: If you cannot go to work on public transport because of your disability you can get three-quarters of the cost of the taxi fares up to a maximum of £65 a week. If you get **Mobility Allowance,** but for some reason cannot drive, your allowance will be reduced by £7.70 a week.

- Rehabilitation courses: There are regular free courses to give disabled people practical work experience and help in looking for jobs, sometimes followed by a three week trial with an employer.

- Sheltered employment: These are special workshops for people who cannot cope with normal work.

● Training courses: The **Job Training Scheme** is open to both disabled and able-bodied people, but disabled people do not have to meet all the conditions set for other people.

● Personal reader service: **Blind** and partially sighted people at work can get help with the cost of someone to read to them part-time for a limited period.

Income Tax for disabled people

There is an extra tax allowance for **blind** people. If you are a married man with children you can get an extra tax allowance, in addition to the ordinary Married Man's Allowance, if your wife is 'totally incapacitated' for a whole tax year. If you support a disabled relative you may be able to claim an extra allowance. *See* **Income Tax** for more details.

If you want to know more

Every disabled person should have a copy of the *Disability Rights Handbook*.

Leaflets:
HB1 Help for handicapped people
HB2 Aids for the disabled
HB4 Help with mobility: Getting around
FB28 Long term sick and disabled: Cash help for people at home

Disabled Rate Relief

If some parts of your home are used to help a disabled person you may be able to get money off your rates. You can get this whether you are a private tenant, a council tenant, or you own your home. This is quite different from an ordinary rate rebate or **Housing Benefit.**

Main conditions

Your home must be the usual residence of a person who is disabled and have facilities which are important to the person because of their disability which affect the rateable value of the home. It doesn't matter whether the facilities were put in specially or not.

Amount

Your rateable value will be reduced, so the amount you benefit will depend on what the value of the facility is and how much your rates are in the pound.

There are standard rateable values for some things.

A room specially for a disabled person, for example a downstairs bedroom, or a room to put special apparatus in £30
An extra bathroom £20
A garage £25
A car port £15
Parking space £5

For other facilities it would depend on what the rateable value was. You could get relief for central heating, space to use a wheelchair in, an extra toilet, a lift or hoist, or anything else which is permanent enough to affect your rateable value and which is important for the disabled person.

How paid

Your rates will be reduced.

How to claim

Get a form from your local council rates department. They will probably want to visit your home. Make sure they do not send you a rate rebate form by mistake.

Age limits

None.

Excluded groups

None. The disabled person does not have to be the ratepayer and does not have to be registered with anyone.

Time limits

You will get rate relief from the start of the rating year in which you apply. There is no other backdating.

Residence requirements

The disabled person must normally live in your home. Temporary absence would not matter.

Means tested

No.

Effect on other benefits

If you get **Housing Benefit** you will get less of it, but the amount you have to pay will go down so it is worth applying.

Effect of going into hospital
Rate relief would not be affected unless the disabled person went away permanently.

Effect of going abroad
The same as going into hospital.

Who administers it
Your local council rates department.

Special tips
In Scotland the way the values are worked out is different, but the principle is the same.

Now that everyone has to pay the first 20% of their rates it is more worthwhile applying for this relief even if you get **Income Support.** There will not be any special relief from the Community Charge or poll tax when that is introduced. *See* **Rates.**

Appeals
If you are refused rate relief you can **appeal** to the County Court within 21 days. In Scotland you appeal to the Sheriff within 42 days.

If you dispute the rateable value of a facility which the valuation officer accepts has a rateable value you can **appeal** about that to the local valuation court.

How to find out more
Books: *Disability Rights Handbook*

Leaflets: Some local councils produce a leaflet.

Law: The Rating (Disabled Persons) Act 1978.

Organisations: This benefit is not well-known. You will be lucky to find anyone who knows much about it outside the local rates department.

Disablement Benefit
see **Industrial Benefits**

Disaster
see **Emergencies**

Disconnection
see **Fuel**

Diseases, industrial
see **Industrial Benefits**

Distraint
see **Debts**

Divorce
see **Single Parents**

Domestic crisis	*see* **Travelling Expenses**
Early retirement	*see* **Retired**
Earnings	*see* **Income**
Earnings related component	*see* **National Insurance Retirement Pension**

Education Benefits

Most of these benefits are discretionary. This means it is up to your Local Education Authority to decide what to provide and how it should be provided. So if you are not happy with the service you should complain to your local councillor.

Free school meals

If you receive **Income Support** then your children are entitled to some sort of free meal at school. It is up to the council what they provide and how.

School uniform and clothing grants

It is up to the council whether they provide any clothing your children need for school. If you think you might be able to get some help apply as soon as you can, because often only a limited amount of money is set aside for these grants.

Educational Maintenance Grants

These are for children who stay at school past the school year in which they become 16. It is up to the council whether to make grants, and if so, how much grant to give. For information on whether children can claim **Income Support** in their own right *see* **Students.**

If your child gets a grant it will not affect your **Income Support.**

If your child is still at school or college, doing work which is not above A level standard, then you may still be entitled to benefits for her or him. *See* **Child Benefit** and **Dependants.** Most widow's benefits allow you to continue to claim for a child until they are 19.

Fares to school

Your children are entitled to free transport to school if the school they have to go to is more than two miles walking distance away if they are under 8, or more than three miles away if they are older. Many local authorities will also provide transport for other children.

Visits to disabled children

If you have a disabled child who is at school away from home the local authority can pay your fares to visit if they choose to.

Claiming

Ask at your child's school, or the education office, about how to claim any of these benefits. If you are turned down you may not have any right of appeal — that's up to the council too.

Educational Maintenance Grant *see* **Education Benefits**

EEC *see* **Abroad; Immigrants**

Elderly *see* **Retired**

Electricity *see* **Fuel**

Emergencies

How to get help when the office is closed

If you contact the police they will be able call the duty number of the **DHSS** and the Social Services in the evening, at weekends or during holidays. There are emergency duty officers who can let you have small amounts of money. In central London there is a special emergency office at DHSS, Keyworth House, Keyworth Street, London SE1. Tel. 01 407 2315.

There are three main ways of getting financial help in an emergency. None of them is easy.

1. The Social Fund

You might be able to get a crisis loan from the **Social Fund** in an emergency, or if you have suffered a disaster, if you can show that it is the only means of preventing serious damage or serious risk to the health or safety of you or your family. You do not need to be getting any other benefit to get a crisis loan.

How much will I get

If you are given a crisis loan for weekly living expenses it will be 75% of your basic **Income Support** allowance, plus £10.75 a week for each child. If you are a **boarder**, a **striker**, or voluntarily **unemployed** there are special rules. The most you can get altogether as a crisis loan is £1,000, and you will not get that much if the **DHSS** think you are not likely to pay it back.

See **Social Fund** for more details.

2. If you have children

The Social Services Department has the power to make payments to prevent the need to take **children** into care. If you are refused help from the **DHSS** and your **fuel** is cut off a social worker may be able to help you.

3. Urgent needs payments of Income Support

If you qualify for weekly payments you will receive a reduced amount of **Income Support.** You can get weekly urgent needs payments in the following circumstances:

● The DHSS are treating you as having notional **income,** but in fact you have not yet got it and you or your family are suffering as a result

● You or your **partner** are a **seasonal worker** and so refused benefit and you are suffering hardship as a result

● You are a person from abroad in certain defined circumstances (this is not a complete list):

    (a) You only have limited leave to stay in the country and your supply of money from aborad has temporarily stopped

    (b) You are not prevented from applying for public funds and you are waiting for a decision to be made about changing the conditions of your stay

    (c) You are waiting for a decision about an appeal

    (d) A decision has been made to deport you but it has been deferred by the Home Office

See **Immigrants.**

How much will I get

If you qualify the amount you get is:

Single people	under 18	£17.46
	18-24	£23.45
	25 +	£30.06
Couple	both under 18	£34.92
	others	£46.31

plus the full amount for your **children,** plus the pensioner premium, if you are old enough, plus your housing costs. From this will be deducted any **income** you have, but you will not be expected to borrow.

Employed

If you are not sure whether you are employed or self-employed *see* **self-employed.**

Benefits while you are working

People who work (or whose **partners** work) full time are excluded from **Income Support** and some other benefits. The rules about what counts as full time vary for different benefits. The benefits which are available to you regardless of whether you are working full time if your income is low (or if you have a lot of children) are:

Legal Aid

Housing Benefit, if you have
   rent or rates to pay

Health Benefits

Emergencies

Education Benefits

Hospital fares

Benefits for **Children** and
   Disabled people

See **DHSS** Leaflet FB 4 Help while you're working.

If you are pregnant *see* **Babies.**

If you are facing **redundancy** *see* that entry.

If you have just started work or want to change jobs *see also* **Work, looking for.**

To claim **Family Credit,** you or your **partner** must be working for more than 24 hours a week and have at least one child.

Benefits for part-time workers

If you have a **partner** who is claiming benefit for you then your part-time work may affect your **partner's** benefit. Look up the rules for the benefit your partner is claiming.

If you are getting a benefit not mentioned here look it up to see if a part-time job would stop you getting it.

Income Support

If you and your **partner** (if you have one) both work less than 24 hours a week you may be able to claim **Income Support** to top up your wages. You may have to show that you are still available to take up a full-time job. If you are **disabled** so that your earning capacity is reduced by at least 25% then you can still claim no matter how many hours you work.

Unemployment Benefit

If you do not work on every day of the week you may be able to claim **Unemployment Benefit** for the days when you don't work. Work on a Sunday will not affect **Unemployment Benefit.** If you regularly work the same hours then your benefit may be stopped because of the Full Extent

Normal Rule (this is explained in the section on **Unemployment Benefit**). Even if you don't get any benefit you may get credited with some **National Insurance** contributions.

Sickness and pregnancy

Statutory Sick Pay and **Maternity Pay** depend on how much you earn, not on how many hours a week you work. If you have more than one part-time job you may be able to get benefits from both employers. If you cannot get SSP or SMP you may be able to get **Sickness Benefit** or **Maternity Benefit.**

If you are getting benefit because you are **sick** or **disabled** then you should check with the **DHSS** and with your doctor before you start doing any regular part-time work, otherwise your benefit might be stopped.

Parents

If you are a parent you may be able to claim **Family Credit** if you work at least 24 hours a week. If you are already getting **Family Credit,** going part-time won't affect your benefit until your order book runs out. There are special rules for **single parents** getting **Income Support** to make part-time work more worthwhile for them.

Starting a part-time job

If you start a part-time job you should carry on signing on as **unemployed** until you are sure you are getting the right benefits. You will have to tell the Unemployment Benefit Office how long you are working and how much you are earning, but you can sign on during the week whenever you like.

Working part-time may affect both your future **Retirement Pension** and any occupational pension you may get. If you are thinking of going part-time you should get **advice** if you think your pension might be affected.

Rights at work

This is a very brief note. If you are having trouble at work you should see your Trade Union, or get **advice** from someone else.

Unfair dismissal

If you have worked for the same employer for more than 16 hours a week for at least two years, or for more than eight hours a week for five years, you may be able to complain to an Industrial Tribunal if you are unfairly dismissed. *See* Department of Employment leaflet 13. If you don't have this right then none of the other rights mentioned are much use to you because if you are sacked for trying to use them there is nothing you can do.

Notice

Once you have been employed for four weeks you are entitled to at least a week's notice of dismissal, unless you are sacked for 'gross misconduct'. After two years you are entitled to two weeks' notice, and from then on you are entitled to a week's notice for each year you have been employed up to a maximum of 12. If you are sacked without the notice you are entitled to be paid for the notice period.

Minimum wages

If you work in some trades and are over 21 you have a legal right to be paid no less than the rate laid down by the Wages Council and it is a crime for your boss to pay you any less.

The main rates for 1988 will be as follows (the rates change at various times through the year. Get **advice** for the up-to-date rates):

Trade	Hourly rate
Shops	£2.33
Hotels and licensed restaurants	£2.00
Cafés and unlicensed restaurants	£2.10
Pubs and clubs	£2.16
Hairdressers	£1.95
Laundry	£2.21
Clothing	£1.99

There should be a notice at the place you work giving the current rates. If you work overtime (over 39 hours for most jobs, but over 40 hours for hairdressing) you are generally entitled to time and a half.

If you have been underpaid you can get money back which you are owed for up to six years. You would need to see a solicitor or get **advice.** In some cities there are Low Pay Units which would help you.

Deductions from pay

Your employer is not allowed to deduct anything from your pay unless there is a law to say he can (this covers **Income Tax** and maintenance arrears), or it says in your contract that he can, or you agree in writing that he can. If you work in the retail trade then no more than 10% can be deducted from any one pay packet. Unfortunately this does not apply to your final pay packet.

Holidays

There is no law which says that you are entitled to a holiday, or to holiday pay. It is entirely between you and your employer. Even Bank Holidays have no law to support them.

Income tax

In some jobs you can claim an extra personal allowance for **Income Tax.** Sometimes there will be a standard amount agreed by a trade union. If there isn't you may be able to get the taxman to agree a special amount for you. You can claim for:

- the cost of replacing or maintaining tools or special clothes which you have to pay for which are only used for your work
- travelling expenses which you have to pay to do your work. You cannot claim for the cost of going to work
- part of the costs of a car if you have to provide one for your work
- professional fees and expenses

There are other ways in which you may be able to reduce the amount of tax you have to pay. For more details *see* **Income Tax.**

Written statement

Every employee (except Crown Servants) who normally works at least 16 hours a week is entitled to a written statement of the terms and conditions of their employment. If you haven't got anything in writing, your employer must give you a statement if you ask for it once you have been employed for 13 weeks. If you think your employer won't want to give you a written statement *see* **Unfair dismissal** above, before you ask. The things the written statement must deal with are listed in Department of Employment leaflet no. 1.

Pay slips

Every employee (apart from the police and sailors) who normally works at least 16 hours a week is entitled to a written pay slip. A list of what must be written on it is given in Department of Employment leaflet no. 8.

More information

There are various leaflets on employment rights you can get from the Jobcentre. You can get **advice** from the Low Pay Unit, or from a trades union. There is a DHSS Leaflet FB 26 Voluntary and part-time Workers — Benefits, pensions and National Insurance Contributions.

Enterprise Allowance

There is a scheme to encourage the growth of small businesses. The purpose is to help unemployed people start up in business without worrying over the loss of their benefit.

Main conditions

- You must be receiving **Unemployment Benefit** or **Income Support** when you apply. No other benefit will do. It is sufficient that your **partner** is claiming for you.
- You must have been unemployed for at least 8 weeks when you apply.
- Your proposed business must be acceptable. Gambling, night-clubs or political or religious businesses will not be supported.
- You must be able to show that you have at least £1000 to invest. That might be an overdraft.
- You must agree to work full-time in the business.

Amount
£40 a week for up to 52 weeks.

How paid
Fortnightly into your business bank account.

How to claim
You can only get an application form by going to an Enterprise Allowance Information Session.

Age limits
You must be over 18 and below pensionable age.

Excluded groups
A business will not be accepted if it is already trading before the start of the scheme, or if it is not independent.

Time limits
The allowance cannot be backdated.

Taxable
Yes — but as part of the business receipts.

Residence requirements
None.

Effect on other benefits
You can get any benefit which you can get as a **self-employed** person at the same time as the allowance. Enterprise Allowance is not treated

as income. It is part of the business. It will be your profit as a whole from the business which will be counted for **means-tested** benefits.

If you fall ill during the 52 weeks you can continue to claim the allowance for up to 8 weeks and then you can claim **Sickness Benefit.**

Additions for dependants
None.

Effect of going abroad
None, so long as you are still working at the business.

Who administers it
Department of Employment.

Special tips
There is no guarantee that you will make any money just because you are accepted onto the scheme. A large proportion of businesses started under the scheme go out of business as soon as the allowance runs out, often leaving the people who started them with large debts. *See* **Debts** for more details.

How to find out more
Jobcentre.
Leaflets: Department of Employment leaflet EPL 124.

Epilepsy	*see* **Disabled**
Equal opportunities	*see* **Disabled** **Women**
Equal treatment	*see* **Women**
Estate	*see* **Death**
European Community	*see* **Abroad** **Immigrants**
Eviction	*see* **Rent**
Evidence	*see* **Appeals**
Exceptionally Severe Disablement Allowance	*see* **Industrial Benefits**

Family Credit

This benefit replaced Family Income Supplement in April 1988.

Main conditions

It is designed for families with children where at least one **partner** is in remunerative work. This means working more than 24 hours a week on average.

Amount

There is a maximum credit for each family. To calculate it take one adult credit (it doesn't matter whether there are one or two adults) of £32.10, and add an amount for each child:

Under 11	£6.05
11-15	£11.40
16 or 17	£14.70
18 or over	£21.35

If your family's net **income,** not including **Child Benefit** or **One Parent Benefit,** is £51.45 or less then you get the maximum. Income is calculated using the same principles as for **Income Support,** but without the disregard for earnings.

If your income is higher than this then deduct 70% of the difference from the maximum to work out what you will be paid.

How paid

You will get an order book, which will last for six months, no matter how your circumstances change. If you wish you can have the money paid directly into a bank account.

Capital

If you have **capital** of more than £6,000 you cannot get Family Credit. If you have **capital** of between £3,000 and £6,000 it will reduce your benefit slightly. If your child has **capital** of more than £3,000 it is excluded from the calculation, but it doesn't affect your benefit otherwise.

How to claim

Form FC1, from post offices or the DHSS. In two parent families the woman is expected to claim. You will need five weekly, or two monthly pay slips, although if you've just started work you should claim first and supply the slips later. If you are **self-employed** you will need some accounts or estimates of what you are likely to earn.

Resident requirements

You must be present and 'ordinarily resident' in Great Britain when you claim. Your remunerative work must all be in Great Britain. If you go **abroad** after you have qualified your benefit will continue until your six months are up.

Taxable

No.

Effect on other benefits

Taken into account in full for **Income Support** and **Housing Benefit.** If you get **Family Credit** you also get **Health Benefits,** free travel to **hospital** for treatment, and you may be in line for **Social Fund** grants for **babies** or funerals (*see* **Death**).

Example:

Clive and Julie have two children aged 12 and 14. Clive's income before tax is £150 per week, and he brings home £115.70.

The maximum Family Credit they could get is £54.90. They would get that if Clive brought home £51.45 or less. In fact he brings home £63.25 more than that, so 70% of the difference (£44.27) is taken off the maximum, leaving them with Family Credit of £10.63 a week.

Who administers it

Family Credit Unit, Poulton-Le-Fylde, Blackpool, FY6 8NW.

Special Tips

If you get Family Credit and pay **Income Tax** as well you will not see more than 19p a week for each £1 a week pay rise. If you get **Housing Benefit** as well you will be on an effective tax rate of 97%.

See also leaflet NI261 A Guide to Family Credit.

Family Fund

This is a Government fund which is administered by the Joseph Rowntree Memorial Trust to help families with severely handicapped children. The child must be under 16 and live in the UK. Although your general circumstances will be taken into account there is no means test.

How to apply

Write to The Family Fund, PO Box 50, York YO1 1UY. Give your name and address, the name and date of birth of the child, the way the child is **disabled,** and the help you need. They will send someone to visit you.

See also **Disabled.**

Fares   *see* **Bus Passes, Disabled, Education Benefits, Hospital, Travelling Expenses, Work — looking for**

Fireman   *see* **Income**

Foreign   *see* **Abroad**
                                               Immigrants

Fraud   *see* **Over Payments**

Free school meals   *see* **Education Benefits**

Fuel

Can't pay your bill?

If you have difficulty paying your fuel bill and you are on **Income Support** you may be able to go on to the Fuel Direct scheme. This means that money is taken out of your weekly benefit and paid directly to the fuel board. The amount deducted will be the board's estimate of your average weekly consumption, plus £1.70 a week towards your arrears. If you are paying more than one bill in this way the most that can be deducted from your benefit for arrears is £3.35 altogether.

Disconnection

The fuel boards have agreed not to disconnect people in the following circumstances:

● The money you owe is not for fuel
● It is between the first of October and the end of March and all the adults in the house are pensioners
● It is safe and practical to put in a slot meter
● You are waiting for a decision from the **DHSS** about whether they will help you

You will not get any help from the **Social Fund** for the cost of fuel or standing charges, except in an **emergency**, but you might get help with the cost of installing a meter or reconnecting the supply.

Severe Weather

If there is a period of exceptionally severe weather, that is an average temperature below freezing point for a whole week, in your area you may be entitled to a payment from the **Social Fund** if you are on **Income Support** and your savings are less than £500.

To qualify you, or someone you claim for, must be over 64, or under 2, or entitled to a disability premium.

You get £5 for each week which is declared officially cold. You only need to claim once and you will be paid for all the qualifying weeks. Get a claim form from your local **DHSS** office.

Full-time education	*see* **Students**
Full-time work	*see* **Employed**
Funerals	*see* **Death**
Garage	*see* **Housing Benefit**
Garnishee Order	*see* **Debts**
Gas	*see* **Fuel**
Giro, missing	*see* **DHSS**
Glasses	*see* **Health Benefits**
Good cause for a late claim	*see* **Backdating**
Government Training Scheme	*see* **Work, looking for**
Graduated Pension	*see* **Retirement Pension**
Grants	*see* **Owner Occupiers, Social Fund, Student Grants**
Green Form	*see* **Legal Aid**

Guardian's Allowance

Main conditions
This is paid to people looking after children who are effectively orphans, either because both their parents are dead or because one is dead and the other at the time of the death was lost or sentenced to more than five years' imprisonment.

Amount
£8.40 per week.

How paid
Order book.

How to claim
Contact your local **DHSS.**

Age limits
Like **Child Benefit.**

Excluded groups
Step-parents do not count as parents so they can claim, but adoptive parents do, so they can't.

Time limits
Claim within three months of being entitled. If you can show good cause then you may be able to get **backdating.**

Taxable
No.

Residence requirements
At least one of the parents must have been born in the UK and spent at least one year in any two year period here since they were 16. There are some special residence rules.

Means tested
No.

Effect on other benefits
Counts as a resource for **Income Support, Housing Benefit** and **Family Credit.** You cannot claim an increase of another National Insurance benefit for a child as a **dependant** and claim guardian's allowance for the same child.

Who administers it
Child Benefit Centre, Washington, Newcastle on Tyne. Tel. 091 416 6722.

Special tips
You don't have to be a child's legal guardian to claim. If you don't qualify but you are looking after someone else's child then you may be able to get a fostering allowance from your local social services department.

How to find out more
Books: *Rights Guide to Non-Means-Tested Social Security Benefits.*
Leaflets: DHSS NI 14
Organisations: *see* **Single Parents.**

Handicapped   *see* **Disabled**

Harrassment   *see* **Rent**

Health Benefits

Prescriptions, dental charges, glasses, milk and vitamins, and help with fares to hospital are all available to some people either free or at a reduced cost. If you cannot get them free for any other reason you may qualify because your income is low. All these benefits calculate what is a low income in the same way. If you don't want to calculate it for yourself just fill in the form and apply anyway.

The government are planning major changes to these benefits and the system of charging for them.

If you get **Income Support** or **Family Credit** you get all health benefits free.

Low income
Work out what your **income** would be for **Income Support.** Do not include any **Housing Benefit.** Then take away the weekly amounts you pay for:

● life insurance
● HP for essential furniture
● your mortgage, rent, and rates (after deducting any **Housing Benefit** you get)

If you have **capital** of more than £3000 you will not qualify.

There is no right of **appeal** if you are refused health benefits because your income is too high, but you could write and ask for an explanation, so you can check if a mistake has been made.

Free Prescriptions

Children under 16, women over 60, men over 65 and women who are pregnant or who have had a baby in the last 12 months all get free prescriptions. Mothers need a form from the doctor or midwife. People who qualify because of their age just sign the back of the prescription.

If you have any of these diseases you are entitled to free prescriptions:

- epilepsy needing continuous therapy
- a permanent fistula
- diabetes mellitus
- myxoedema
- hypoparathyroidism
- hypopituitarism
- Addison's disease and other forms of hypoadrenalism
- myasthenia gravis
- any physical disability which stops you going out alone.

War pensioners can get free prescriptions for their war injuries.

You qualify for free prescriptions because of low income if your net income as worked out above is not more than £3.50 above your requirements for **Income Support.** If you need more than one item on your prescription you are allowed an extra £2.20 on your income for each extra item. Remember that if you are over 16 it is your own income which counts.

How to claim

Apply on form P11 from the post office or chemist if you are not in one of the categories where you are allowed just to sign the back of the prescription.

If you can't get free prescriptions it may still be worthwhile buying a season ticket if you think you will need more than 15 prescriptions in a year.

Dental treatment

Dental treatment and false teeth are free to everyone under 18, to those under 19 who are in full-time education and to women who are pregnant or have a child under 1. Just tell the dentist you want free treatment.

If you get free prescriptions because of low income you can get free dental treatment too. You will have to fill in a form at the dentist's.

Otherwise work out your income using the formula above. If it is no more than £2.50 above your needs for **Income Support** you will get free treatment. Otherwise you may get a reduced charge. You can only be asked to pay three times the amount your income exceeds the free treatment level. Any charges you have to pay within three weeks are added together and count as one charge.

Dental examinations are free to everyone at the moment, but the Government plan to introduce charges for those not entitled to free treatment. The amount mentioned is £3, but the charge will probably not be introduced until 1990.

If you think you might get some help fill in form D11 from the dentist or the post office.

Glasses

Anybody can get a sight test free. Charges may be introduced in 1990. The optician must give you your prescription, and you can take it elsewhere to have your glasses made.

NHS glasses have been abolished, but you may be able to get a voucher to help you to pay for new glasses.

Who can get a voucher for glasses?

These people can get the voucher automatically. Just tick the box on the sight test form.

- Anybody under 16
- Students under 19 in full-time education
- Anyone who gets **Income Support** or **Family Credit**
- Anyone who gets other health benefits free because of low income.

If you think you have a low income get form F1 from the optician. Fill it in and send it to the **DHSS**. The optician will give you a voucher, but you cannot use it until the **DHSS** send back form F3(O) to tell you how much your voucher is worth.

See also leaflet G11 NHS vouchers for glasses.

If you are prescribed certain very powerful glasses, either by the optician or the hospital, you get given a voucher automatically.

What do you do with the voucher?

If you are under 16 or registered blind or partially sighted you must take your voucher to an optician. Otherwise you can take your voucher to any shop which supplies glasses. You can put extra money to it to buy any glasses you want.

Repairs

People under 16 can get their glasses repaired under the NHS. Everybody else has to pay for their own repairs.

Milk and Vitamins

- Disabled children who are not at school can get free milk between the ages of 5 and 16. Get form FW20 from the **DHSS**.
- Day nurseries, childminders and playgroups can get ⅓ pint of milk a day for each child they look after. Contact the social services office.

● If your family get **Income Support** then any pregnant woman or nursing mother you claim for and each child up to 5 years and 1 month (or until the child starts school, if that is later) should get milk tokens and vitamins automatically. If you aren't getting yours then tell your local **DHSS**. If you are owed milk tokens from more than four weeks ago then you should get cash instead.

What do you get?

If you qualify you get 2 bottles of children's vitamin drops every 13 weeks, 2 containers of vitamin tablets every 13 weeks for pregnant women and a total of 5 containers for nursing mothers and a pint of milk a day for every adult or child who qualifies. Babies under 1 get 2 packs of dried baby milk each week.

If you don't qualify you should still be able to buy dried milk and vitamins at maternity clinics and child health centres.

If you want to know more

There are more details in the *National Welfare Benefits Handbook*. A health visitor or midwife is probably the best person to ask for advice. *See* leaflet MV11 free milk and vitamins.

Hearing
see **Disabled**

Heating
see **Fuel**

Holidays
see **Employed, Family Fund, Income, Income Support, Unemployed**

Home Improvement Grants
see **Owner Occupiers**

Home Office
see **Immigrants**

Home ownership
see **Owner Occupiers, Rates**

Home responsibility protection
see **National Insurance**

Homelss

If you are homeless and

- you have children, or
- you are over pensionable age, or
- your family includes a person who is pregnant, or physically or mentally **disabled,** or vulnerable in some other way

your local council is obliged to help you, unless they think you have become homeless intentionally. If you think that your council should help you and they won't then you need to get **advice** from someone who specialises in this area of the law. A housing advice centre, a law centre or a solicitor who does this kind of work should be able to help you.

Benefits for homeless people

There is no legal reason why homeless people shouldn't get any benefits they are otherwise entitled to, and most of the benefits in this book are not restricted to people with a fixed address. In practice, however, homeless people have a great deal of difficulty. There are two main reasons.

The most important reason is that **DHSS** consider that homeless (or nomadic) people are particularly likely to claim benefit fraudulently. Homeless people very often have difficulty proving who they are, because many of the documents which settled people use to prove their identity, like rent books and bank cards, are not available to them. If you are moving around you will find it a lot easier if you can keep with you some sort of identity document with your picture on it.

The other reason, which does not affect the **DHSS** so much as other organisations, doctors in particular is that if you don't have an address then you don't belong to any particular area. This gives any official who wants it the perfect excuse — 'You're not my problem'.

Income Support for homeless people

If you have no accommodation you are entitled to your personal allowance. If you are unemployed you have to sign on every day to collect your benefit, although you can argue for weekly payments.

You can also get a voucher for board and lodging. *See* **Boarders.**

Social Fund

You may be able to get a loan for **rent** in advance, and a loan or grant for furniture.

Other Benefits

If you are homeless and **sick** or **disabled** then you may be able to get some other benefit which will be less trouble than **Income Support.**

Hospital

Effect of being in hospital

If you go into hospital most benefits will be reduced after a time, usually to £8.25, the hospital pocket money rate. **Family Credit, Mobility Allowance, Statutory Sick Pay** and **Statutory Maternity Pay** are not affected if you go into hospital. The effect on other benefits depends on how long you are in hospital and what your family situation is. After four weeks **Attendance Allowance** stops.

After six weeks

For **Sickness** and **Invalidity Benefit, Severe Disablement Allowance** Widow's Benefits and **Retirement Pension** your benefit will be reduced by £16.50 if you live alone, or if you and your **partner** are both in hospital, and by £8.25 if you have a partner or **dependants.**

For **Income Support** a single person will just get £8.25 plus housing costs. A **single parent** will continue to get dependant's addition, family and other premiums as well. A couple's benefit will be reduced by £8.25, unless both are in hospital. A single **boarder** can get retaining fees paid if they are likely to return to their accommodation when they come out of hospital. Premiums and additions for dependant **children** will continue for everyone so long as some members of the family are not in hospital.

After twelve weeks

If your child is in hospital you would only lose **Child Benefit** and dependant's additions to most benefits if you were not incurring expenditure for the child — such as not visiting. If you are on **Income Support** you only get £8.25 for the child. Disabled Child Premium, however, continues as does Family Premium, so long as you are responsible for the child.

After 52 weeks

The benefits which were reduced at six weeks are now cut to £8.25. If you are single with **dependants** £16.50 will be paid to your dependants. A couple on **Income Support** is treated separately at this stage, but may be treated separately at an earlier stage. The **partner** in hospital gets £8.25 and the remaining partner must make a separate claim. *See* **Partner** for more details.

If a person is a long-stay patient who sometimes comes out of hospital, for example on weekend leave, they can claim **Income Support** for the time they are out.

See also leaflet NI9 Going into Hospital?

Coming out of hospital

If you have been in hospital for a long time, or if your living condtions are likely to lead to your going into hospital you may be able to get a grant or loan from the **Social Fund** for furniture, repairs, removal expenses, or other payments which will help to keep you out of hospital.

Hospital fares

There are different rules for claiming help with the cost of going to hospital depending on whether you are visiting a patient or if you, or someone you claim for, is going for treatment.

There are special arrangements for people who live in the Scottish Highlands and Islands or in the Isles of Scilly.

Fares for Patients
Main conditions

You can claim whether you are going to stay in the hospital or if you are just going for an appointment. If you are in hospital you can get your fares to come home.

If you get **Income Support** or **Family Credit** you qualify automatically. If you are not on those benefits you might qualify if you are not very well off.

Amount

You get the cost of the cheapest form of public transport. If there isn't any public transport where you live you get the cost of a taxi to the nearest place where there is public transport. If you claim for the cost of going by car you will get the cost of the petrol.

If you need someone to go with you their fares can be paid too. You would need a letter from a doctor to prove this. If your child has to go to hospital then you can get the cost of transport for an adult to go with them.

If you think you need an ambulance you must tell the doctor. You cannot claim for this.

How paid

Usually you have to pay the fares yourself and claim a refund. If you need the money in advance the **DHSS** can give you a travel warrant, but they will need at least three days' notice to do this.

How to claim

If you have an order book for **Income Support** or **Family Credit** you just show it to the receptionist or social worker at the hospital. You might need to keep your ticket to show them too. They will give you the money that day.

If you don't have an order book you need to claim on form H11 and send your claim to your local **DHSS**. Use the form whether or not you are getting any benefits. The hospital may be prepared to ring the DHSS to confirm you are on benefit and pay you straightaway.

Time limits

It's best to claim at least a week before you go, but you can still claim even if you have already been and come back. You might be able to claim arrears if you haven't claimed before.

Taxable

No.

Means tested

If you are not on **Income Support** or **Family Income Credit** there is a separate means test. *See* **Health Benefits.**

Earnings rule

If your income is low you can still claim even if you are working.

Effect on other benefits

None. But there are special benefits for **war pensioners** who go into hospital for their war disability.

Who administers it

Partly the hospital and partly the local **DHSS** office (or the **Family Credit** office, if you get that).

How to find out more

Books: *National Welfare Benefits Handbook; Disability Rights Handbook.*

Leaflets: H11 Fares to Hospital.

Law: National Health Service (expenses in attending hospitals) Regulations.

Organisations: Hospital social workers are usually the only people who really understand this system.

Fares for visitors

You may be able to get a grant from the **Social Fund** to visit someone who is ill in hospital or a home if you are on **Income Support** and you don't have enough savings over £500 to pay the cost yourself. Normally the patient should be a close relative or a **relative** who doesn't have other visitors or someone who was treated as part of your family. The patient will be expected to contribute if they or you get more than hospital pocket money for them. You can also get a grant to visit someone who is not in hospital, but is critically ill, or for your children to go and stay with someone while you are in hospital.

Hospital fares	*see* **Hospital**
Hospital pocket money	*see* **Hospital**
Hostels	*see* **Boarders**
Hotels	*see* **Boarders**
Hot water	*see* **Fuel, Housing Benefit**
Household	*see* **Partner**
House maintenance	*see* **Owner Occupiers**

Housing Benefit

Main conditions

You must have either rent or rates to pay on your home — or both. You need not be the tenant or ratepayer. If the person who should pay is not doing so, perhaps because they are away, then you can get help if it is reasonable to give the help to you. Rental for boats and caravan sites is included. If you are *not* on **Income Support** then you can get Housing Benefit to help with the rent even if you live in a hostel or in bed and breakfast (*see* **Boarders**).

You can get benefit for a period of up to four weeks before you move into a new home if

- you are moving out of hospital or a home
- you had to wait for adaptations for a **disabled** person in your family
- you were waiting for a decision on a **Social Fund** payment and you are **disabled** or retired and have a child under 6

If you have to pay for two homes, perhaps because you are moving. or having repairs done, you can get benefit for both for up to four weeks if you can show that you have to pay for both places. If you left your last home because of domestic violence or the threat of it then you can get benefit for two homes for as long as the council think it reasonable. There are special rules for **students** with two homes.

Residence requirements

You must normally occupy the home you are claiming for. Unless you have moved out for repairs to be done you will not be able to claim Housing Benefit if you occupy another dwelling anywhere in the world. If you are temporarily away, even if you are abroad, you can still get Housing

Benefit for up to a year so long as you lived in your home before you
went away and you do not intend to be away for more than a year and
your home has not been let.

There are special rules for **Students.**

Subtenants and boarders

If you have subtenants then what your subtenants pay you is counted
as **income.** The first £4 a week is disregarded and a further £6.70 if their
rent includes fuel. The main differences between subtenants and **boarders**
is that boarders get some food as part of the deal and the income from
boarders does not count as **income.** Boarders are counted as **non-
dependants,** so they will affect your benefit, but not nearly as much.

How Much

The most you can get is your whole **rent** and 80% of your **rates.** You
get that if you are on **Income Support,** or if your income is no more than
it would be if you were on it. If you get **Income Support** then your benefit
includes £1.30 a week (£1 if under 25) to compensate you for having to
pay the first 20% of the rates yourself.

Rent does not include

- the cost of **fuel.** If fuel is provided but no specific charge is made for
  it the Council will deduct £6.70 for heating, £0.80 for hot water, £0.50
  for lighting and £0.80 for cooking. Heat and light of common areas,
  like the stairs in flats are counted in as rent.
- meals
- laundry (the provision of laundry facilities is counted in)
- leisure items, sports facilities, television rental and licence fees (the
  cost of a children's play area is allowed)
- cleaning your own accommodation, unless no-one in your household
  is capable of doing cleaning
- transport
- furniture or equipment if it is to become yours
- nursing, medical or personal care
- counselling or support services unless they are provided by the landlord
  in person, or by someone whose main job is connected with the
  building, like a caretaker.

Rent levels

If the Council think you are trying to fiddle the system they can refuse
to pay you *any* Housing Benefit. If they think your rent is too high, or
your home too large, they can limit the amount they pay, but they should
only do this if there is somewhere cheaper which is suitable, taking into
account the nature, facilities and security of tenure of your present home.
Only if you are old or disabled or have children do they have to show

that this cheaper accommodation is available to you and consider whether it is reasonable to expect you to move, bearing in mind jobs and schools. They have to take all the personal circumstances of you and your family into account. The policy which some councils have of refusing to pay rent over a certain limit without taking all the circumstances into account is illegal.

See **Rent** if you think your rent is too high, or if you are having trouble with your landlord. If your rent goes up too much, or more than once within a year, the Council can refuse to pay the increase.

Later in 1988 the Government intend to bring in new controls on the level of rent which can be met by Housing Benefit. Rent Officers will decide whether the rent you pay is reasonable, although they will no longer have the power to fix a rent for new tenants. They will also decide if your home is too large for the size of your family. They will only decide whether you get Housing Benefit for the whole amount of the rent. If you do not cooperate with the Rent Officer you will not get any benefit. Councils will be prevented from paying Housing Benefit for the most expensive rented properties in their area.

How to Claim

Get a form from your local Council or Housing Office. If you claim **Income Support** you will get a Housing Benefit claim form NHB1 enclosed.

Age limits

None.

Excluded groups

People whose **capital** is worth more than £6,000. **Students** from abroad, and students living in college property.

People who own their own houses, Crown tenants, and people who live in co-ownership schemes, can only get help with the **rates.**

Time limits

Housing Benefit can be **backdated** for up to a year. You have to show that there is a good cause for your failure to claim at the right time.

Taxable

No.

Means tested

Yes. The rules are complicated. If you don't want to work out how much you will get just apply to the Council and ask them to explain how they've worked out your benefit. They don't usually get the sums wrong but they often put the wrong information about you into their computer. If you want to work it out for yourself this is how its done:

Housing Benefit Calculation

You claim for yourself and your family if they live with you. Family includes your **partner** and your children, so long as you get, or should get, **Child Benefit** for them.

The first step is to calculate your *applicable amount* in the same way as for **Income Support,** but with the difference that

- the **single parent** premium is £8.60 instead of £3.70
- there is no allowance for the cost of a mortgage

Then calculate your **income,** including the same disregards as for the other **means-tested** benefits, and the same tariff income if your capital is over £3,000.

If your income is *less* than your applicable amount then you get the maximum Housing Benefit — all your rent, as calculated above, and 80% of your rates.

If your income is *more* than the applicable amount then you lose 65p from your rent rebate and 20p from your rate rebate for each pound a week you have over the applicable amount.

If there is anyone in your home who you are not claiming for you then have to take a deduction from your benefit for their contribution to the house. *See* **Non-dependants.**

Hospital

Your applicable amount is reduced if you are in **hospital** for more than six weeks, so your Housing Benefit may be reduced along with any other benefits you get. *See* **Hospital.**

Extra Housing Benefit

If your circumstances are exceptional the Council has the power to pay you extra Housing Benefit up to the whole cost of your **rent** and **rates.** If you think that your circumstances are exceptional you should write to the Council and say so. They will want to know how your circumstances affect your ability to pay the rent and rates.

Appeals

You are entitled to a written notice of every decision the council takes about your Housing Benefit within 14 days of their receiving all the necessary information. If you don't give them all the information they ask for within 4 weeks of being asked for it they don't have to make a decision. The decision has to tell you what information about you it is based on. You are also entitled to a written explanation of how your benefit has been worked out, which must be sent to you within 14 days of your asking for it. If you are unhappy with any decision the council has made about your benefit you should write and ask them to explain their decision. If you are still unhappy with their explanation ask them to reconsider. They must consider what you write and write back to you within six weeks. If you are still unhappy then you can **appeal** within 28 days to a Housing Benefit Review Board.

Housing Benefit Review Board

You are entitled to a review by the Review Board if you write back to the council within 28 days of their reply to your asking them to reconsider. When you write you must explain why you want a review. There should be a hearing within six weeks.

The Review Board consists of three councillors from the council for your area, so its independence from the decision you are complaining about is questionable. Apart from that it is very like an appeal tribunal. You have the right to present witnesses and documents to the Board, and to question the council officer who puts their case. You can have a friend or representative with you if you want to. You should get at least two weeks' notice of the hearing. You are entitled to a written decision. There is no right of appeal against the decision of the Review Board.

How is Housing Benefit paid?

Usually every two or four weeks, either by cheque, by giro, direct to your bank account or straight to your landlord. The council 'must have regard to your reasonable needs and convenience', and if your benefit is more than £2 per week you can insist on being paid every two weeks.

Council tenants and ratepayers are always paid by direct credit to their accounts with the council, so no money changes hands. If you have signed something to say that the money should be paid to a private landlord then you can change your mind at any time. If you are more than 8 weeks in arrears with your rent, or they think it in your interest, or if you have moved out the rent can be paid direct to the landlord without your consent. If the Council think that you are not paying your rent to your landlord they can withold your Housing Benefit.

If you live at an unsafe address where mail goes missing you should ask the council if you can arrange to come in and pick up your money.

If you have just made a claim and you need your money urgently then ask the council for an interim payment if they can't pay you your full benefit straight away. If you are on **Income Support** the council have to make a payment within two weeks of being told to by the **DHSS**.

How to find out more
Leaflets:
RR1 Help with Housing Costs
RR2 A Guide to Housing Benefit (from council offices)

Ignorance   *see* **Backdating**

Ill   *see* **Sick**

Immigrants

The law which affects the right of people from abroad to claim benefits is highly complicated. It is also one of the few areas of Social Security where you can do yourself serious and irreparable damage by doing the wrong thing. If you, or someone you are trying to help, has recently come from abroad then you should get **advice** *before* you approach the **DHSS.**

There are two questions which people from abroad have to think about. The first is 'Am I entitled to claim a benefit?' The second is 'If I claim this benefit will it harm my immigration status?'

If a person is admitted to the country with a condition that they 'do not have recourse to public funds' then they could put their right to stay here in danger if they claim **Income Support, Housing Benefit, Family Credit,** or housing provided for **homeless** people.

The people who are admitted to the UK with the condition that they must not claim public funds are:

- visitors and working holidaymakers
- fiancés and fiancées
- **students** and their **dependants** (but students' dependants can claim **Housing Benefit)**
- **dependants** of work-permit holders
- religious ministers, business people, and people of independent means
- wives and children of persons settled here on 1st January 1973.

If a person has a **partner** who is not in one of these categories then the partner may be able to claim for the two of them.

Many people from abroad can claim **Income Support,** or payments from the **Social Fund** in an **emergency,** but to do so may harm their immigration status.

People from abroad who can claim **Income Support** normally without worrying about the effect it might have on their immigration status are:

- people with a right to stay in the UK permanently
- people who have been granted refugee status or political asylum.

If you are not in one of those categories then get **advice** before you claim **Income Support, Housing Benefit, Family Credit,** or housing provided for **homeless** people.

Other benefits
The rules for claiming other benefits if you have come from abroad are given individually for each benefit under the heading **Residence conditions.**

The DHSS and the Home Office
There are close links between the **DHSS** and the Home Office. If you are not sure whether you have a legal right to stay in the UK you should not claim any benefit until you have got **advice,** because you will be interviewed and your claim will be reported to the Home Office if you have settled in the United Kingdom in the last five years. The DHSS may ask you for your passport to prove that you have a right to be in the country. If you have one and it is in order it may be quicker to produce it to sort out your claim.

To find out more
There is a useful book called *Immigrants and the Welfare State,* published by the National Association of Citizens' Advice Bureaux. There should be a copy in every CAB. It is now out-of-date. *See also* the *National Welfare Benefits Handbook. See also* **Abroad.**

Improvement Grants   *see* **Owner Occupiers**

Incapable of work   *see* **Invalidity Benefit**

Income

1. Earnings
Even benefits which are not **means-tested** are affected if you earn more than a certain amount, although they are not affected by other income you might have, such as income from savings. The amounts are different for each benefit, but the way the amount is calculated is the same for all the benefits which are not means-tested. The calculations are different for **Family Credit, Housing Benefit** and **Income Support.** The rules that follow are in two parts.

If you are **self-employed** then it is particularly difficult to work out what you earn. See that entry for more details.

Non-means-tested benefits
The figure the **DHSS** use when they calculate your earnings for non-means-tested benefits is your weekly earnings *before* tax but *after* the

deduction of **National Insurance** contributions and some other expenses. Occupational pensions count as earnings.

Any money or perks from your employer counts as earnings except:

● Meals provided at work
● A house or flat that you have to live in to do the job
● Food or other goods for your use
● Luncheon vouchers up to 15p a day
● A Christmas bonus

You can deduct from your gross earnings:
● **National Insurance** contributions (but not **Income Tax**)
● Trade Union subscription
● Fares to and from work
● The cost of making reasonable provision for looking after another member of your household (for example **childminding)**
● Overalls or other work clothes and the cost of cleaning them
● Tools or equipment. If you are **self-employed** this might include the cost of somewhere to work
● Any other reasonable expense

It is up to you to work out your earnings (and sometimes those of your **partner**) and tell your local **DHSS** if they are more than the limit in any week. If you don't do this you may have an **overpayment** which you might have to repay if it is discovered.

Means-tested benefits

The rules for **Family Credit, Housing Benefit** and **Income Support** for earned income are slightly different from the rules above. The most important difference is that you can make more deductions from your gross earnings, so that the figure the **DHSS** use is much closer to the amount that you actually receive, but you can't deduct the sort of expenses which you have to pay for yourself.

The following all count as earnings:

● Bonus or commission
● Payment in lieu of notice from full time work
● Holiday pay, unless received more than 4 weeks after the end of the job
● Retainer
● Payment of 'unnecessary' expenses by your employer, such as childcare or travel to work

An advance of wages, or a loan, or 'legitimate' expenses, or payment in kind, will not count as earnings. Nor will earnings of a child, unless the child has left school.

You can then deduct:

- **Income Tax**
- **National Insurance** contributions
- Half of any pension contributions
- 'Necessary' expenses — such as travel while at work, or the cost of cleaning overalls.

If your income is not constant it will be averaged, normally over five weeks or two months depending how you are paid.

For **Income Support** and **Housing Benefit** £5 of each person's earnings will be disregarded. For some people a higher disregard applies. These are:

- People who are **disabled** and are entitled to the disabled premium
- **Single parents**
- A person who works as a part-time, auxiliary or reserve in the fire service, coastguard, lifeboat or armed services.

The higher disregard is £15 and it applies to a family. No couple can ever have more than £15 of their joint income disregarded. For **Income Support** a couple can also qualify for the £15 disregard if they have been on **Income Support** or Supplementary Benefit continuously for two years as a couple (not necessarily the same couple) and during that two years neither of them has been working or been in full time education. For Housing Benefit there is a £10 disregard of earnings for a couple if they don't qualify for the £15 disregard.

2. Other income

Only **means-tested** benefits are affected by income which is not earned, although occupational pensions count as earnings for some purposes.

If you or any member of your family receives any voluntary or charitable payment which is not regular the first £250 in any year is treated as **capital.**

The following do not count as income:

- expenses paid by a charity or voluntary body, if you receive no other payment from them
- expenses paid by your employer for necessary expenses
- **Housing Benefit**

- **Mobility Allowance**
- **Attendance Allowance**
- George Cross or Victoria Cross payments
- Educational Maintenance allowances
- any part of a **student grant** which is intended for fees, books etc
- travelling allowances paid by the MSC to a person on a training course
- Job Start Allowance
- the first £5 a week of any voluntary or charitable payment if not paid by a liable relative
- the first £5 a week of any **war pension** or war widow's pension, or pension for victims of Nazi persecution, so long as you don't benefit from the treatment of voluntary payments above
- interest paid out of a home income plan
- the first £35 a week from each **boarder**
- any income in kind
- any income paid outside the UK which you cannot bring into the country
- any payment for fostering, adopting or being custodian of children, or for caring for someone who doesn't normally live with you
- payments from a mortgage protection policy during the operation of the 16 week rule
- any payment made to you which is intended and used for housing costs or mortgage capital repayment

Income Support

How this article is arranged

The peculiarities of how Income Support affects particular groups of people are explained under the headings:

- **Boarders**
- **Children**
- **Disabled**
- **Employed**
- **Immigrants**
- **Owner Occupiers**
- **Prisoners**
- **Retired**
- **Seasonal Workers**
- **Self-employed**

- **Sick**
- **Single Parents**
- **Strikers**
- **Students**
- **Unemployed**
- **Women**

What is Income Support?

Income Support is the official poverty line laid down by Parliament as the amount of money you need to live on. If you get Income Support, even if it is only a few pence, you are automatically entitled to claim **Health** and **Education Benefits,** and after six months you are eligible for loans from the **Social Fund.**

Who can claim Income Support?

Income Support is paid to families, not to individual people. A family can be a single person living alone or a woman and a man and any children living with them who are under 16 or under 18 and still at school. If you have a **partner** you will have to decide which one of you should claim. *See* **Women.**

Age

To make a claim you must be over 18, unless you can persuade the DHSS that you will suffer severe hardship if you are not allowed to claim in your own right. The rules for when people leaving school or college can claim are under **Students.**

Residence

You must be in Great Britain. *See* **Immigrants** for the problems of people who have recently come from abroad. If you go abroad temporarily your Income Support will stop if you have to sign on as **unemployed** to get it (although you can go to Northern Ireland for 4 weeks). If you do not have to sign on as unemployed your benefit generally continues for the first four weeks.

Remunerative Work

If your or your **partner** are in remunerative work you cannot claim. 'Remunerative' means more than 24 hours a week on average and done in the expectation of payment. This rule does not apply to **disabled** people whose earning capacity is reduced by at least 25%.

You are still treated as being in remunerative work:

- if you are off work because of a holiday. If you have no holiday pay you may be able to claim as an emergency
- if you are away from work without a good reason. If you are on strike *see* **Strikers**

Part-time work

If you work part-time you will have to sign on as **unemployed** to get Income Support, unless you fit into the list of people who don't have to sign on.

Do you have to sign on?

This is a list of situations in which you don't have to sign on to get your benefit:

- over 60
- **single parent,** or a single person looking after foster children
- **sick** and incapable of work
- looking after a child because the person who usually looks after him is ill or temporarily away from home
- caring for someone who gets or has claimed **Attendance Allowance**
- within 11 weeks of having a baby, or seven weeks after, or incapable of working because of pregnancy
- **disabled** and your earning capacity is reduced by at least 25%
- **blind** or recovered your sight in the last 28 weeks
- a refugee who is learning English for the first nine months
- a **student** who is disabled, estranged, an orphan or a single parent
- on an MSC scheme **(Youth Training Scheme)**
- women over 50 and men over 55 who haven't worked, or signed on, for the last 10 years and have no prospects of work
- Open University Summer School
- required to go to court for more than two days
- a **prisoner** released in the last seven days or still remanded in custody

How to claim Income Support

If you are **unemployed** you get a form B1 from the Unemployment Benefit Office. Otherwise contact your local **DHSS** office. They will send you a form. They are very long forms, but you will not have to answer all the questions.

Answer the questions carefully. You can get **advice** to help you fill it in. You will find that some of the questions are not for you, and you will be told on the form not to answer them. If you miss out any questions that do apply to you the **DHSS** will send the form back to you. You should send the form back filled in as soon as possible. *See* **DHSS** for some tips on how to deal with the local office.

Giving information to the DHSS

The law is that if you want benefit you have to show the **DHSS** any document they reasonably ask for. If you unreasonably fail to provide information they will send you a form to say that your claim will be cancelled if you don't give them the information they want within 21 days.

You cannot appeal against this. If you think they are being unreasonable, because, for example, you don't have the information they want, you should write back and say so. You can ask them to make a decision using the information they already have. If they decide that you aren't entitled you can then **appeal.**

Claims from other people
If you give someone else authority in writing they can make a claim for you. If someone is not capable of acting for themselves, for example because they are too old or too ill, the **DHSS** can appoint someone to claim for them.

Backdating your claim
Normally you will not get benefit for any day before the date of your claim, so you should not delay. There are four reasons which will enable your claim to be **backdated.** It is up to you to ask for it to be backdated. The four reasons are:

● You were waiting for a decision on another benefit. This includes waiting for your employer to make a decision about **Statutory Sick Pay** or **Statutory Maternity Pay.** You must claim as soon as you get the decision, and your benefit should be backdated to the date you claimed the other benefit. There is nothing to stop you claiming before the decision on the other benefit comes.

● You are waiting for a decision on **Housing Benefit.** Your Income Support will be backdated to the date of your claim for Housing Benefit if you claim Income Support within a month of the Housing Benefit decision.

● Your Income Support stopped when you were in **hospital.** If you claim within three weeks of coming out it will be backdated to the date of your discharge.

● You have good cause for a late claim (*see* **Backdating**).

How your Income Support is worked out
You qualify for Income Support if your **income** is less than the amount set for a family like yours. You get the difference. If you were getting Supplementary Benefit on 10th April 1988 and you have been getting Income Support continuously since then you will not get less than that amount. *See* **Transitional Protection.**

There are special rules for people who are **Boarders, Homeless, Prisoners** or **Strikers.** *See* those headings.

How much do you need to live on?
The amount you need to live on, known as your *applicable amount,* is divided into three parts:

1. *Personal Allowance* — based on age

Single, under 18	£19.40
Single 18-24	£26.05
Over 25	£33.40
Single parent under 18	£19.40
Single parent over 18	£33.40
Couple, both under 18	£38.80
Couples generally	£51.45

If you have children add an extra amount for each child

Under 11	£10.75
11-15	£16.10
16 or 17	£19.40
18	£26.05

2. *Premiums*

(a) Family premium   £6.15
You get this if there is a child in your family, regardless of what other premiums you get.

(b) Disabled Child Premium   £6.15
If you have a child who gets **Attendance Allowance, Mobility Allowance** or is registered **blind** and does not have more than £3,000 **capital.**

(c) You get the highest one of the following which you qualify for:

(i) Disability Premium   Single £13.05   Couple £18.60
You, or your **partner,** must be under 60 and meet one of the conditions:
- gets **Attendance Allowance**
- gets **Mobility Allowance** or equivalent
- gets **Invalidity Pension** or **Severe Disablement Allowance**
- registered **blind**
- claimant is treated as having been **sick** for at least 28 weeks

(ii) Lone Parent Premium   £3.70

(iii) Pensioner Premium   Single £10.65   Couple £16.25
You or your **partner** must be over 60

(iv) Higher Pensioner Premium   Single £13.05   Couple £18.60
You or your partner must be over 80, or under 80 and over 60 and
- meet the conditions for the Disability Premium, or
- met those conditions within eight weeks of your 60th birthday and have been getting Income Support ever since

Once you are getting one of these premiums if you lose your entitlement for less than eight weeks your premium will not be affected.

(d) Severe disability Premium   Single £24.75   Couple £49.50
You must meet all the conditions:

- getting **Attendance Allowance** (both of you, if you have a **partner)**
- for either you or your **partner** no-one gets **Invalid Care Allowance**
- no **non-dependant** living with you unless they are also getting **Attendance Allowance,** or they are a **boarder,** or a carer supplied by a charity

3. *Housing requirements*
   If you are an **owner occupier** your housing requirements (money for your mortgage or service charges), apart from your **rates,** are paid to you as part of your Income Support. Rent and rates are dealt with by the local council. *See* **Housing Benefit.** You are expected to pay water rates yourself, unless you get **Transitional Protection.** If there is anyone else in your home who is not in your family, such as a grown-up child, a **boarder,** an elderly **relative,** or a friend, they will be treated as a **non-dependant** and expected to pay a share of the costs of the home. You will also have a deduction if you have tenants or subtenants. *See* **Housing Benefit** for the details.

How to work out your resources for Income Support

If you have **capital** worth more than £6,000 you cannot get Income Support. If you have capital worth more than £3,000 the **DHSS** will assume that you get an **income** of £1 per week for each £250 above £3,000.

If you have any **income** it will be counted from the day it is due to be paid to you, and taken into account for as long as the period it was for, although there are special rules for your last pay packet from work. So if you get paid monthly the payment will be taken into account for a month from the day it is due.

See **income** for the details of how to calculate your income.

Payment of Income Support
The decision

The **DHSS** should make a decision whether or not to pay you within 14 days of the time when they have all the information they need. If you need money before that you may be able to claim as an **emergency.** You should get the decision in writing. If you get a payment you should receive a small form, How Your Benefit is Worked Out. You can get a more detailed explanation if you ask for it. You need it if you want to check that you are getting the right money. DHSS often make mistakes.

If you get a decision that you are not entitled to any benefit, or not as much as you think you should get, you should consider an **appeal.**

Paydays

Income Support is paid on a weekly basis. If you have to sign on as **unemployed** you will be sent a giro every two weeks. Most other people will be given an Order Book. You will start to get your benefit from your first payday, which is decided by your surname or by the day your pension is paid. You might have up to six days between the day you claim and your payday. If you need money before your normal payday you must claim as an **emergency.** No-one will tell you this. You are expected to ask.

Deductions from your benefit

If you are in **debt** you can arrange for some of your benefit to be paid to the person you owe the money to. Sometimes this can be done without your consent. *See* **Fuel** for the rules about this.

Stopping your money

If the DHSS think you may not be entitled to benefit they can suspend your payments. *See* **Overpayments** for what you can do if this happens.

Lost giros

If a giro doesn't arrive *see* **DHSS** for what to do. If you live at an address where mail often goes missing you can arrange to pick up your giro from the Unemployment Benefit Office or from the DHSS.

How to find out more

Leaflet SB20 A Guide to Income Support.

Income Tax

This is only a very brief note on income tax, as it affects those with very little money. It does not deal with the problems of people who are **self-employed** or earn more than £10,000 a year.

Personal allowances

Everyone is allowed a certain amount of income each year without having to pay tax on it. This amount is your *personal allowance*. The amounts change every year in the budget. The figures I am using are those for 1987/88, but the figures for any other year will be different. Years for tax purposes start on 6th April and last until the next 5th April. If you do not earn as much as your personal allowance in the year you will not have to pay any tax. If your income is more than your personal allowance you will have to pay tax on every pound over the level of the allowance.

If you are a married man and your wife works your allowance will be higher than hers. If she is paying tax and you are not it is possible to transfer some of your unused tax allowance to her so that she pays less tax without you paying any more.

Married man's allowance

In 1987/8 a single person's allowance is £2425 for the year. Everyone should get a single person's allowance automatically. A married man's allowance is £3795 for the year. You still count as a married man for the year in which your marriage ends. If you are separated from your wife but fully supporting her of your own free will (that means without a court order or legal agreement) you still qualify for the married man's allowance. If you get married during the year you get 1/12th of the allowance for each month after you are married until April.

Single parents

If you are not legally married you cannot get the married man's allowance, but **single parents** get an allowance which is the equivalent. An unmarried couple with two children could each get the additional allowance and so be better off than a married couple in the same position.

A widow or widower can claim an extra allowance of £100 for a live-in housekeeper. If you are a widow or widower with children you are better off claiming the **single parent's** allowance.

Other allowances

People who are over 65 can claim an additional age allowance. There is a further allowance for people over 80. *See* **Retired.**

Registered **blind** people can claim a small allowance.

If your wife is 'totally incapacitated' for the whole of a tax year you can get the additional personal allowance if you have children as well as the married man's allowance. *See* **Disabled.**

If you are old or disabled and you support your son or daughter who lives with you to look after you then you can claim an additional allowance of £55 a year.

If you support a relative who is old or disabled and whose income is no more than a basic **Retirement Pension** you can claim an extra allowance of £100 a year. Single women can claim £145 a year.

Tax allowances for mortgages or loans to improve property are dealt with under **Owner Occupiers.**

Tax relief on maintenance payments is dealt with under **single parents.**

Tax relief on expenses at work is dealt with under **employed.**

How to claim tax allowances

Unlike social security, your tax affairs can be adjusted for past years. If you have paid too much tax you can get a refund for the last six tax years (if you have paid too little you may have to pay extra tax for the last six years).

If you think you are entitled to some extra allowance write to your tax office. If you are working this will probably be the office which deals with your firm's head office. If you are unemployed it will be your local tax office. If you have a disagreement with the tax office you can appeal, but get **advice** before you do. Mistakes can be expensive.

Tax and benefits

Although many benefits are taxable (and the Government plans to increase the number that are) you don't normally have tax deducted from your benefit. If you have tax to pay it will be deducted from your other income. If you are unemployed you will not be able to claim a tax rebate if you are claiming benefit until the end of the tax year or when you start a new job, because your benefit will be using up your personal allowance. If your taxable benefits come to more than your personal allowance then you may be liable to pay tax at the end of the year, and this would normally be collected when you start work. For this reason it is important to check your tax allowances even if you are not working. One thing worth checking is that **Income Support** paid to unemployed people is taxable, but **Income Support** paid for any other reason isn't.

Advice about tax

If you cannot afford to employ an accountant you can get advice from the PAYE Enquiry offices which have been established in many big towns. Although you won't be able to talk to your own taxman you will be able to get general advice. To find the nearest one *see* 'Inland Revenue' in your telephone book.

Books

There are lots of books about taxation, but most of them are designed for rich people. Probably the best cheap guide is the *Daily Mail Income Tax Guide,* by Kenneth R. Tingley. It cost £1.75 for the 1986/7 edition.

Incontinence   *see* **Disabled**

Independent student   *see* **Student Grant**

Industrial Benefits

Benefits for people and their dependants who suffer because of industrial accidents and diseases are a very old-established part of the social security system. There are a lot of complexities and the sections which follow only give an outline of the system. The advice, as usual, is that if you think you might be entitled then you should claim, and carry on claiming until you are convinced that you have got all you are entitled to. Many people who are entitled don't claim what they are entitled to, and lose a lot of money as a result. It can make a difference of more than £100 a week, if you suffer a serious injury, for you to qualify for Industrial Benefits rather than ordinary benefits.

The benefits listed below are not directly paid by your employer. If you think that your injury or disease might have been caused by your employer's negligence then you should consider claiming **compensation** from your employer as well. If you are in a trade union you should consult them. They will have experience in dealing with the sort of problems which occur in your sort of work. You will probably need a solicitor if your problem is at all serious, and you should choose one who is experienced in 'personal injuries'. You must normally claim within three years of the event.

See **Disabled** for details of other benefits which are available to all disabled people.

Who is covered by the Industrial Injuries Scheme?

Anyone who is employed and pays, or ought to pay, Class 1 **National Insurance** Contributions is covered. You are still covered even if your wages are so low that you do not pay any contributions, or if you pay the 'married woman's stamp'. Some other people are included although they are not employees. These include:

- apprentices
- mine inspectors and rescue workers
- special constables
- some offshore oil and gas workers
- taxi drivers
- office cleaners
- agency workers
- ministers of religion
- lecturers
- airmen and mariners

If you are **employed** by your spouse or by a close **relative,** or if you are a member of visiting armed forces, you may not be treated as employed.

Self-employed people are not covered. They are expected to arrange their own insurance.

If you are a trainee on an MSC course, such as the YTS, you are covered by the MSC Industrial Injuries Scheme, which pays benefits which are very similar to those in the Industrial Injuries Scheme.

What injuries and diseases are covered by the scheme?
A. Diseases

There is a list of nearly 60 different diseases which are recognised as being caused by work. The list is in leaflet NI.2. It includes such well-known conditions as miner's lung and farmer's lung. There are conditions caused by heat, vibration, radiation and repetition of movement. Deafness is included. There is a list of diseases which are caught from animals, and a long list of diseases caused by industrial poisons, including certain cancers, certain asthmas and asbestosis. There are special rules for pneumoconiosis and byssinosis.

You have to show not only that you suffer from the disease in question but also that you have worked in the job which causes it. For most of the diseases if you can show both of these things it is presumed that the work caused the disease if it developed while you were working or shortly after. For asthma you must have worked in the job within the last ten years and for deafness within the last five years.

B. Accidents

You have to show that your injury was caused by an accident 'arising out of and in the course of your employment'. Sometimes this is obvious, but there are many books of arguments about cases which are not obvious.

'Injury' includes psychological injuries and diseases as well as broken arms and legs. 'Accident' cannot include something you do deliberately, but it might include something someone else does to you deliberately, such as when a teacher is beaten up by pupils.

Most accidents which happen at work are covered by the scheme, and you may be covered even on your way to work or on the way home, especially if the accident happens on the firm's land, or in a bus which they have arranged. If your accident happened while you were doing something quite unconnected with your work, such as going out to place a bet, you are not covered, unless you are going to help in an emergency.

This book does not deal with all the benefits related to disability. There are a number of benefits which have now been abolished, and if you have trouble with one of them you will need specialist **advice**.

What benefits can you claim under the Industrial Injuries Scheme?

If you cannot work because of an industrial injury or disease you can qualify for **Sickness Benefit** and later **Invalidity Benefit** even if you haven't paid any **National Insurance** Contributions.

If you suffer from any disability caused by an industrial injury or disease which lasts for more than three months you may be entitled to Disablement Benefit. Unless you suffer from pneumoeoniosis, or a similar disease, you will only get paid any benefit if you are at least 14% **disabled.** You can still get this benefit if you are working. If your disability affects your earning power you may qualify for Reduced Earning Allowance, even though you are less than 14% disabled and do not get any other benefits.

If your disablement is 100% you may be entitled to Constant Attendance Allowance. You may also get Exceptionally Severe Disablement Allowance, but as you do not have to claim that separately there are no details about it in this book.

If your husband dies because of an industrial accident or disease, you can qualify for Widow's Benefit even if he had not paid sufficient **National Insurance** contributions.

Appeals

If you are refused benefit or disagree about the amount of your award you can **appeal** to the Social Security Appeal Tribunal. There are special procedures for dealing with medical questions about these benefits, such as what disease you are suffering from and how disabled you are. Appeals against questions of that sort are heard by the Medical Appeal Tribunal. Their main job is to give you a medical examination, rather than to listen to your arguments.

Disablement Benefit
Main conditions

You must suffer a 'loss or physical or mental faculty' as a result of an industrial accident or disease which happened, or began, at least 90 days ago.

Amount

Up to £67.20 per week for 100% disability. If your disability is assessed as less than 14% you don't get the benefit unless your disability is due to pneumoconiosis, byssinosis or diffuse mesothelioma. If your disability is between 14% and 20% you get the 20% rate, which is £13.40 per week.

How paid

Weekly order book or direct credit transfer. You may be awarded benefit for life or for a specified period.

How to claim

Get a form from your local **DHSS.**

Age limits

None, but there are reduced rates for people under 18 without dependants.

Time limits

You can get benefit **backdated** for three months. If you can show good cause you can get it backdated indefinitely, without the usual twelve month limit.

Taxable?

No.

Residence requirements

No.

Means tested

No.

Earnings rule

None. The question of whether you are capable of work is a separate and independent question. *See* **Reduced Earnings Allowance** in this article.

Effect on other benefits

Taken into account in full for all **means-tested** benefits, although you may qualify for a premium if you are **disabled.**

Additions for dependants

None.

Effect of going abroad

None.

Who administers it

Local **DHSS.**

Special tips

If your condition gets worse you can ask for a review, even if you weren't awarded a pension previously.

Leaflets

NI6 Disablement Benefit and Allowances
NI2 Industrial Injuries: Prescribed Industrial Diseases
FB15 Injured at Work
NI3 Industrial Injuries Benefit Paid for Pneumoconiosis and Byssinosis
NI207 Occupational Deafness
NI223 Prescribed Diseases: Notes for Medical Practitioners
NI226 Pneumoconiosis: Notes on Diagnosis
NI237 Occupational Asthma
NI238 Clinical Notes on Occupational Asthma

Reduced Earnings Allowance

Main conditions
- You must be disabled because of an industrial disease or injury, and
- you must be assessed as more than 1% disabled, and
- because of that either
  a) you are never able to go back to your normal job or do another job for the same money, or
  b) although you have gone back to your normal job you have had to give it up, and you are never likely to be able to go back to it, or to do work of an equivalent standard.

You may be able to claim if you lose your prospect of promotion because of your disability.

Amount
Maximum £26.88 a week.

How paid
Weekly order book.

How to claim
Contact your local **DHSS.**

Age limits
When you retire you get Retirement Allowance instead. This is 25% of the Reduced Earnings Allowance you were getting.

Excluded groups
The same as **Disablement Benefit** above.

Taxable
No.

Earnings rule
The purpose of Reduced Earnings Allowance is to compensate for earnings you have lost because of your disability. The money you could earn in your old job is compared with what you could earn now. You get the difference, up to the amount of the maximum. Most people get the maximum.

Effect on other benefits
Paid on top of other industrial benefits, but you cannot get more than 140% of the full rate of Disablement Benefit when you add this to your Disablement Benefit.

Additions for dependants
None.

Effect of going abroad
Benefit continues, normally for three months so long as you are not going abroad to work.

Who administers it
Local **DHSS.**

Constant Attendance Allowance

Main conditions
You must be assessed as 100% disabled because of an industrial accident or disease (or under the **War Pensions** scheme) and get Disablement Benefit because of this. You must need daily attendance.

Amount
Normal maximum: £26.90
Part-time rate: £13.45
Intermediate rate: £38.70
Exceptional rate: £53.80

How paid
By order book.

How to claim
Local **DHSS.**

Age limits
None. There is a lower rate of £41.15 for people under 18 without **dependants.**

Time limits
You must claim within three months of becoming entitled. You can get **backdating** if you can show good cause.

Taxable
No.

Means tested
No.

Earnings rule
None.

Effect on other benefits
None.

Additions for dependants
No.

Effect of going abroad
Still paid for six months at least.

Who administers it
Local **DHSS.**

Special tips
Don't confuse with ordinary **Attendance Allowance.** You can't have both. Constant Attendance Allowance is easier to qualify for, and is more valuable. If you get it you may also get Exceptionally Severe Disablement Allowance.

Appeals
You have no right of appeal about any decision on this benefit.

How to find out more
Leaflets:
FB15 Injured at work
N16 Disablement Benefit

How to find out more
For all Industrial Benefits:

Books:
Ogus and Barendt; Disability Rights Handbook; Rights Guide to Non-Means-Tested Social Security Benefits; Compensation for Industrial Injury, Richard Lewis, Professional Books, 1987. (This is a thorough and scholarly treatment of the subject, and not easy reading.)

Organisations:
Trade unions are usually the best source of advice. Some hospital social workers may develop expertise if their hospital specialises in relevant conditions. There are a number of support groups for people suffering from particular conditions. Some illnesses are practically confined to small communities of people who work in the same industry. General advice agencies outside of these communities are unlikely to get much experience with the problems.

Insulation   *see* **Owner Occupiers**

Interest on loan   *see* **Owner Occupier**

Intermediate Grant   *see* **Owner Occupiers**

Interview   *see* **Work, looking for**
                                                         DHSS

Invalid Care Allowance

Main conditions
You must be caring for a person who gets **Attendance Allowance** or Constant Attendance Allowance. You must care for them every day of the week and for at least 35 hours during the week.

Amount
£24.75 per week.

How paid
By weekly order book or credit transfer.

How to claim
Form NI212 from your local **DHSS.**

Age limits
You must be over 16 and normally under pensionable age.

Excluded groups
People in full-time education or who are 'gainfully employed'.

Time limits
Claim within three months. If you can show good cause then your benefit can be **backdated.** If you have claimed **Unemployment Benefit** or **Income Support** when you should have claimed Invalid Care Allowance then your claim can be **backdated** to the time when you claimed the wrong benefit.

Taxable?
Yes, but it can be offset against the married women's earned **income tax** allowance.

Residence requirements
You must be ordinarily resident in Great Britain and have been here for at least 26 weeks in the last twelve months.

Means tested
No.

Earnings rule
You lose the benefit if you earn more than £12 per week unless it is during your 'holiday'.

Contribution test
None.

Effect on other benefits
Counts in full as income for **means-tested** benefits.

Additions for dependants
£14.80 for a wife or husband who is not earning more than that amount, £8.40 for each child.

Effect of going into hospital
You lose the benefit if you are in hospital for more than 12 weeks. If your patient loses **Attendance Allowance** because they are in hospital for more than four weeks (or for any other reason) then you lose your benefit.

Effect of going abroad
A temporary absence from the UK of not more than four weeks does not affect your benefit. If your patient goes abroad and their **Attendance Allowance** continues then you can go too and your benefit will continue. You aren't treated as abroad if you or your patient are in the forces.

Who administers it
ICA Unit, Norcross, Blackpool. Tel. 0253 856123.

Appeals
To the Social Security Appeal Tribunal.

Special tips
Married women can claim Invalid Care Allowance but if you are looking after your husband who gets **Invalidity Benefit** and he gets a **dependants'** increase for you, or if he gets **Income Support** for the pair of you, you won't get any more money by claiming ICA, but you will protect your pension and your independence.

Once you have started getting the benefit you can have a break of up to 4 weeks holiday every six months.

How to find out more
Books:
Rights Guide to Non-Means-Tested Social Security Benefits
Disability Rights Handbook

Leaflets: NI212

Organisations: *see* **Disabled**

Invalidity Benefit

Main conditions

You must be incapable of work and have used up your entitlement to **Sickness Benefit, Statutory Sick Pay** or **Maternity Benefits** since you last worked. This means that you may go straight on to Invalidity Benefit if you are unemployed for some time and have previously used up your entitlement to the other benefits. Invalidity Benefit normally starts six months after you became incapable of work.

For advice about what to do if the **DHSS** think you are not ill enough to carry on getting benefit *see* **Sick.**

Amount

£41.15 per week plus an Invalidity Allowance which depends on how old you were when you stopped work.

Invalidity Allowance

Age when you stopped work		amount
men	**women**	
under 40	under 40	£8.65 a week
40-49	40-49	£5.50 a week
50-59	50-54	£2.75 a week

You may be entitled to an additional earnings related pension. *See* **National Insurance** Contributions for details of how it is calculated. Your Invalidity Allowance will be reduced by the amount of any additional pension you get. If you are over pensionable age it will also be reduced by the amount of any occupational pension you get.

How paid

Usually by weekly order book or credit transfer.

How to claim

Send your medical certificate from the doctor to your local **DHSS.** If you have been getting **Sickness Benefit** you will automatically be transferred on to Invalidity Benefit. If you have been getting **Statutory Sick Pay** your employer should give you a form SSP 1 (T) for you to send to the **DHSS.**

Age limits

If you get Invalidity Benefit before you retire you can, if you wish, carry on getting it until you are 70 if a man or 65 if you are a woman, instead of **Retirement Pension.** Although **Retirement Pension** is paid at the same rate it is taxable.

Excluded groups

- If you are incapable of work because of misconduct. For example alcoholism is an illness, but drunkenness is misconduct.
- If you fail to attend a medical examination without good cause.
- If you refuse treatment without good cause.
- If you behave in a way which will stop you getting better.
- If you go away from home without saying where you are going.
- If you work other than 'therapeutically'. *See* **Earnings rule,** below.

Time limits
You may be able to get **backdating** if you can show good cause.

Taxable
No.

Residence requirements
None.

Means tested
No.

Earnings rule
The only work you are allowed to do is:

- Work under medical supervision while you are a patient which forms part of your treatment.
- 'Therapeutic' work, designed, for example, to keep your mind off your illness. Before you try any work you should make sure that both your doctor and the **DHSS** know and approve, or your benefit may be stopped.

In either case you must not earn more than £27.00 per week.

Contribution test
You must pass the contribution test for **Sickness Benefit** unless you are a widow or a widower, for whom there are special rules, or if you are suffering from an industrial injury or disease.

Effect on other benefits
Counted in full for **means-tested** benefits.

Additions for dependants
Yes. You can claim an extra £24.75 a week for a wife or husband if they are not earning more than £32.75, and an extra £8.40 per child, subject to the amount of your partner's earnings. *See* **Dependants.**

Effect of going abroad
Benefit normally continues.

Who administers it
Local **DHSS.**

Special tips
Many unemployed people are entitled but do not realise that all the periods of illness they have had since they stopped work are added together to meet the six month rule.

How to find out more
Books:
Rights Guide to Non-Means-Tested Benefits, Smith and Rowland.
The Law of Social Security, Ogus and Barendt.
Disability Rights Handbook, Robertson.

Leaflets: NI16A

Organisations: There are organisations for the sufferers from many diseases who may be able to help. Hospital social workers may also help.

Investments	*see* **Capital**
Isle of Man	*see* **Introduction; Abroad**
Isles of Scilly	*see* **Hospital**
Jobclub	*see* **Unemployed**
Job hunting	*see* **Work, looking for**
Job Introduction Scheme	*see* **Disabled**
Jobstart	*see* **Work, looking for**

Job Training Scheme

This is an MSC scheme for people who have been **unemployed** for at least six months, particularly those under 25. You get an MSC allowance which is the same as the **Income Support** you got when you were unemployed, and you get the same **Housing Benefit** too.

It is planned to amalgamate this scheme with the **Community Programme** in September 1988. At the time of writing it is expected that there will be a premium of £10 a week above the rate of benefit you were getting before you went on the scheme. There will also be an allowance for **childminding** of up to £50, and payment of your travel costs above £5 a week.

Key money	*see* **Social Fund**
Kidney dialysis	*see* **Disabled**
Late claims	*see* **Backdating**
Law	*see* **Books** **Legal Aid**
Law Centres	*see* **Advice**

Leaflets

All the leaflets mentioned in this book should be available from any Citizens' Advice Bureau. If no other address is given they are also available from the **DHSS**. If you have difficulty getting them, or you want a lot, you can get them from DHSS Leaflets Unit, PO Box 21, Stanmore, Middlesex HA7 1AY. Leaflets about going abroad come from Overseas Branch, DHSS, Newcastle upon Tyne, NE98 1YX. There is an order form in FB2 Which Benefit?

Leaving a job	*see* **Unemployed**

Legal Aid

There are 3½ different kinds of legal aid:

1. Legal Advice and Assistance. This covers advice and help with any legal problem, but not normally the cost of going to court. There is a scheme which covers assistance by way of representation, under which a solicitor can be paid to represent you in family cases in the Magistrates' Court, before Mental Health Review Tribunals and before boards of Prison Visitors.
2. Civil Legal Aid. This covers going to court to present your case.
3. Criminal Legal Aid. This covers the cost of your defence if you are charged with a crime.
3½.The £5 fixed fee interview. Most solicitors will give you half an hour or so for £5 — often for nothing. This is really just enough time to decide whether you have a case which is worth taking on, and to see how much it might cost to do it.

Legal Advice and Assistance
Main conditions

You must need advice or help about a question of English Law. There are separate systems of legal aid in Scotland and Northern Ireland.

Amount

£50, or £90 if you are starting an undefended divorce. This will pay for between 2 and 4 hours of a solicitor's time. The solicitor can ask for an extension (more money) if your problem is particularly complicated.

How paid

To your solicitor.

How to claim

Make an appointment with any solicitor in the legal aid scheme. The solicitor has to fill in the claim form (the green form).

Age limits
None. Children under 16 normally apply through their parents, but they can have advice or help personally if necessary.

Excluded groups
A solicitor can refuse to give you advice and does not have to give you a reason. If you have had advice and assistance from another solicitor about the same thing you must tell any other solicitor you go to. S/he will have to ask permission from the Legal Aid Office before giving you any more help or advice.

Time limits
Your solicitor won't get paid for any work done before the green form is signed.

Residence requirements
No.

Means tested
There are two tests, one for savings and one for income. You have to pass both. If you are married and live with your partner the income and savings of both of you will be added together unless you have different interests in the question you want advice or help about.

Savings rule
Add up all your savings. Don't count your house or things you use, or the value of the thing you want advice about. Add up the number of people who depend on you (usually your partner and children, if you have any). From the value of your savings deduct £200 if you have one dependant, £320 if you have 2 dependants, £380 if you have three dependants and another £60 for each extra dependant. This is your disposable **capital.** If it is more than £800 you will not qualify.

Income rule
If you pass the savings test you are automatically eligible if you get **Income Support,** or **Family Credit.** Otherwise your solicitor will take your actual income over the last seven days after tax and **National Insurance** Contributions and take off £29.70 for your wife or husband (if you are living together) or the maintenance you have paid over the last seven days (if you are living apart), and the following amounts for dependants:

under 11	£13.00
11-15	£19.50
16-17	£23.45
over 18	£30.45

There are allowances for your rent, rates and mortgage. What's left is your disposable income. If it is under £55 you will not have to pay anything. If it is over £117 you will not get any help. If it is in between you will have to pay a contribution of between £5 and £65.

Normally your solicitor will expect you to pay your contribution at once, but you can pay in instalments.

Effect on other benefits
None.

Who administers it
The Regional Legal Aid Office. Your solicitor will normally deal with them.

Special tips
If you recover or preserve any money or property using legal advice and assistance then normally the solicitor will be paid out of that, unless it would cause great hardship or distress, or if the sort of property makes it difficult. So if you recover a small sum, or a pet, the rule would not usually be applied. Money will not be recovered out of:

- maintenance payments
- up to £2500 in a matrimonial property settlement
- payments under affiliation orders
- social security benefits
- your house or furniture
- half of any **redundancy** payments

Appeals
None. But if you don't get advice from one solicitor you can try another.

Civil Legal Aid

Main conditions
This is to cover cases in the civil courts, where disputes about divorce, children and money are heard. You cannot get help to conduct a case involving libel or slander, and you cannot get help for representation at an inquest or before most tribunals (you can get legal advice and assistance about these).

Amount
There is no limit on the amount you can have, but the legal aid office have to agree that it is reasonable to grant you legal aid. They will balance the amount which you are going to court for against the likely cost of the court case and its importance to you.

How paid
To your solicitor.

How to claim
Your solicitor will help you to complete the form. It may take several

months before you get a decision, but if the matter is urgent you can get emergency legal aid granted by telephone. Sometimes you will get a legal aid certificate which will pay for your case to be taken to a certain stage, such as getting a barrister's opinion, and it will then be reviewed.

Age limits

None.

Time limits

Your solicitor will not be paid for any work he does before your legal aid certificate is granted, so there will be a wait of several months before anything happens.

Means tested

Your income and your savings will be examined by the **DHSS.** You have to pass the test on savings and on income. Work out your savings by adding up all the money you have, whether invested or not, including the surrender value of life assurance policies and the value of any property you own. Do not count the value of your home or your personal possessions, or anything which is the subject of the case. If your savings are less than £3000 you will not have to pay a contribution from your savings. If your savings are more than £4710 you will not normally be granted civil legal aid unless your case is going to be very expensive. You may be asked to contribute up to the balance of your savings over £3000. If you have to pay from your savings you normally have to pay when you get the offer of the legal aid certificate.

Income rule

Work out your weekly income including any benefits you get apart from **Housing Benefit, Attendance** and **Mobility Allowance.** Include your partner unless the case is against them.

Deduct **Income Tax, National Insurance Contributions,** pension contributions, any maintenance you pay, fares to and from work, trade union subscription, the cost of childcare while you are at work, and the cost of your rent and rates (after **Housing Benefit**), mortgage, ground rent, service charges and water rates. Then take off the same fixed amounts as for dependants when calculating entitlement to legal advice and assistance above, £1.95 if you own your home.

The figure you get is your weekly disposable income. Multiply it by 52 to get your yearly disposable income. If it is under £2325 you don't have to contribute anything out of your income. If it is over £5585 you don't qualify. In between you have to pay a contribution.

Contribution

The highest contribution you can be asked for from your income is ¼ of the amount by which your yearly disposable income is greater than

£2325. If you have to pay from income you normally pay in 12 monthly instalments, the first when you accept the offer of the legal aid certificate.

Who administers it

The Regional Legal Aid Office.

Special tips

If your financial position changes while you are getting legal aid your case will be reviewed.

If you win your case you normally have to pay back the cost of your legal aid from what you win. You should check with your solicitor how much is being spent at each stage of the case, because if you win you will have the bill to pay. There are some exceptions to this rule.

Appeals

If your application is turned down you usually have the right to appeal to the Area Committee.

Criminal Legal Aid

Main conditions

It is up to the court where you are charged to decide whether it is in the interests of justice that you should be represented and that you need help to meet the costs. The chances of getting criminal legal aid vary enormously from court to court.

You should be more likely to be granted criminal legal aid if you are likely to go to prison or lose your job, if your case is legally complicated, if you do not speak English well, or if you are mentally ill. Courts vary in the importance they attach to these things.

How it works

If you are questioned about a crime by the police you are entitled to free legal advice without any means test. You don't have to have been arrested or taken to a police station.

If you have to go to a magistrates' court for a criminal charge there will usually be a duty solicitor there who will represent you on your first appearance without any cost or means test.

You can get legal advice and assistance about a criminal matter (*see* above).

Criminal legal aid covers the cost of preparing your case, defending you in court, and, if necessary, appealing. There is no limit on the amount you can have; it is up to the court to decide.

How paid

To your solicitor.

How to claim

Get an application form as soon as possible after you have been charged from the court which is dealing with your case. If you are refused you can apply again, and keep on applying up to the time of the trial.

Age limits
If you are under 17 your parents or guardian can apply for you.

Means tested
If the court decides that you can afford it you may have to pay a contribution. You will not have to pay a contribution if you are getting **Income Support** or **Family Credit,** or if your disposable income (as calculated for civil legal aid, above) is less than £46 a week. If it is more than £46 a week you will be asked to pay ¼ of the amount over £46 every week for six months. If you have any savings over £3000 you will be asked to pay the amount over £3000.

If you do not pay your contribution, without telling the court, your legal aid will stop.

Who administers it
The court where you are charged.

Special tips
If you are found not guilty you usually get your contribution back.

Appeals
For more serious cases you can **appeal** against a refusal of legal aid to the Criminal Legal Aid Committee of the Law Society.

How to find out more
Books: Full details are in the *Legal Aid Handbook,* published every year by HMSO.

Leaflets: The Law Society Legal Aid Guide available from Legal Aid Head Office, Newspaper House, 8-16 Great New Street, London EC4A 3BN.

Liable relative   *see* **Single Parents**

Libraries   *see* **Advice**

Lifeboat   *see* **Income**

Living together	*see* **Partner**
Local office	*see* **DHSS**
Local ombudsman	*see* **Advice**
Lodger	*see* **Boarders**
Lone parent	*see* **Single Parents**
Lost Giro	*see* **DHSS**
Lost money	*see* **Emergencies**
Lost papers	*see* **DHSS**
Low pay	*see* **Employed**
Lump sum	*see* **Capital**
MSC	*see* **Community Programme, Work, looking for**
Maintenance	*see* **Owner Occupiers, Single Parents**
Mandatory Grant	*see* **Student Grant**
Married Man's Allowance	*see* **Income Tax**
Married women	*see* **Partner, Women**
Maternity	*see* **Babies**

Maternity Allowance

Main conditions

You must be unable to get **Statutory Maternity Pay.**

You can get benefit for up to 18 weeks continuously. You are entitled to take 13 weeks starting with the 6th week before your baby is due but you can take the other five weeks either before, or after, or some before and some after.

Amount

£31.30 a week.

How paid
Weekly order book.

How to claim
Get claim form MA1 from the **DHSS** or antenatal clinic and send it to your local DHSS. You will need a certificate giving your expected date of confinement. If your employer has refused to give you **Statutory Maternity Pay** he should have given you form SMP1 which you should send in with your claim.

Time limits
You must claim within 4 weeks of being entitled, unless you can show good cause for a late claim (*see* **Backdating**).

Taxable
No.

Means tested
No.

Earnings rule
You cannot get benefit for any day when you work.

Contribution test
You must have worked and paid standard rate **National Insurance** Contributions for at least 26 weeks out of the 52 weeks ending with the 15th week before your baby is due.

Effect on other benefits
You cannot get this together with any other Contributory Benefit. It counts in full for **Income Support** or **Housing Benefit,** but it would be ignored for **Family Credit** because it only lasts a short time. If you do not qualify for Maternity Allowance you might qualify for **Sickness Benefit.**

Additions for dependants
You can claim an addition of £19.40 for an adult **dependant.**

Effect of going abroad
Benefit will continue during a temporary absence from the country if you go for treatment for an illness which began before you went.

Who administers it
Local **DHSS** office.

How to find out more
Books: *Rights Guide to Non-Means-Tested Social Security Benefits.*

Leaflets: FB8 Babies and Benefits. NI 17A Maternity Allowance.

Maternity Grant	*see* **Babies**
Meals allowance	*see* **Boarders**

Means-tested

Means-tested benefits are those where you have to prove how poor you are before you can get them. The main means-tested benefits are:

- **Income Support**
- **Housing Benefit**
- **Family Credit**
- **Health Benefits**
- **Student Grants**
- **Legal Aid**

Medical Appeal Tribunal	*see* **Appeals**
Member of Parliament	*see* **Advice**
Mental handicap	*see* **Disabled**
Mental illness	*see* **Sick**
Meters	*see* **Fuel**
Milk & vitamins	*see* **Health Benefits**
Minimum wages	*see* **Employed**
Misconduct	*see* **Unemployed**
Missing Giros	*see* **DHSS**

Mobility Allowance

Main conditions

You must be physically disabled. Mental disability counts if it is caused by some physical condition. This means that Downs Syndrome children can often qualify.

You must be unable to walk

or

virtually unable to walk

or

the effort of walking would be a serious danger to you.

If you have artificial aids, such as a false leg, or built up shoes, it is your ability to walk using them that is measured.

Virtually unable to walk means that you cannot walk out of doors without severe discomfort for enough distance or at enough speed or for a long enough time or in a reasonable manner. If you cannot walk a hundred yards without having to stop then you will probably qualify.

It is not just people who have trouble with their feet and legs who get this allowance. If you have a serious problem with your lungs, heart, chest or blood it may be dangerous or impossible for you to walk very far.

Where you live cannot be taken into account. If you live five miles from the nearest bus stop that doesn't make any difference.

Amount

£23.05 a week.

How paid

By order book every 4 weeks, or by direct transfer to your bank account. You can use your allowance to buy a car under the motability scheme.

How to claim

Use leaflet NI211 and send it to the **DHSS** in Blackpool. They will arrange a medical examination. If you cannot get to the doctor the doctor will come to you.

Age limits

You must be over 5 and under 66 when you claim. If you get the allowance you may keep it until you are 75.

Time limits

The allowance cannot normally be **backdated.** Your condition must be likely to remain the same for at least a year.

Taxable

Not since 1982.

Residence requirements

You must be usually resident in Great Britain and have been here for at least 52 weeks in the last 18 months.

Means tested

No.

Effect on other benefits

Mobility Allowance is not taken into account for any other benefit. If you get it, you are entitled to a number of other fringe benefits. See **Disabled.**

Effect of going into hospital

You can keep your benefit provided you can still benefit from it. In practice you only lose your benefit if you are in a coma or are unable to be moved for medical reasons.

Effect of going abroad

Benefit will continue for the first 26 weeks of a temporary absence abroad, and longer if you go abroad for medical treatment.

Who administers it

DHSS Mobility Allowance Unit, Norcross, Blackpool FY5 3TA. Tel. 0253 52311.

Special tips

If your inability to walk is caused by a war injury there is a special scheme. The allowance is paid at a higher rate, there is no upper age limit and you can carry on getting it for life.

Appeals

If you are turned down you appeal first to a medical board of two doctors, who will give you another examination. If they turn you down as well you can appeal to a Medical Appeal Tribunal, which is made up of a lawyer and two consultants. You should get **advice** before you go to a Medical Appeal Tribunal. There is a right of appeal against the Medical Appeal Tribunal to the Social Security Commissioner.

If you are turned down you can apply again, as often as you like.

How to find out more
Books:
Disability Rights Handbook
Rights Guide to Non-Means-Tested Social Security Benefits

Leaflets:
NI211 Mobility Allowance
Door to Door Guide. Dept. of Transport complete rundown on everything
you might need to know if you have difficulty getting around, whether
or not you get Mobility Allowance. *See* **Disability** for the address.

Organisations:
The Disabled Drivers' Association, The Hall, Ashwellthorpe, Norwich,
NR16 1EX. Tel. 050 841 449
Disabled Drivers' Motor Club, 1a Dudley Gardens, London W13 9LU.
Tel. 01 840 1515
Mobility Advice and Vehicle Information Service, Department of Trans-
port, TRRL, Crowthorne, Berkshire RG11 6AU. Tel. 0344 779014
Motability, Boundary House, 91-93 Charterhouse Street, London EC1M
6BT. Tel. 01 253 1211

Money lost   *see* **Emergencies**

Mortgage   *see* **Owner Occupiers**

Moving house   *see* **Social Fund**

National Insurance

Your contributions pay not only for National Insurance Benefits but
also towards the cost of the Health Service, and the Maternity Pay fund.
It is only for benefits that your individual contribution record is important. Your contributions are counted by years. The years are the same
as tax years — from April to April.

There are four classes of contributions. The question of which class you
should pay is decided by the **DHSS.** Until 1977 married women could
choose to pay a reduced contribution (the married woman's stamp). Married women who were paying the reduced stamp at that time can carry
on doing so if their circumstances don't change, but the small contribution
they do pay entitles them only to **Industrial Benefits.** *See* leaflet NI1 for
married women.

There are leaflets for a number of special occupations explaining the National Insurance position:

War Pensioners	NI50
Mariners	NI24
Company Directors	NI35
Share Fishermen	NI47
Examiners, part-time teachers etc.	NI222
People who work for overseas employers	NP16
People who work for agencies	NI192

FB14 is a general explanation of the system of National Insurance — with pictures!

The four classes of National Insurance Contribution are:

● Class 1 Contributions

Paid by employees and their employers if the employee is normally resident in Great Britain, and is between the ages of 16 and pensionable age.

If you earn less than the lower earnings limit (£41 a week in 1988/9) you do not pay.

Contracted in rates

These are for people who will get a state earnings related pension.

Weekly pay	Employee	Employer
£41-£66.99	5%	5%
£67-£104.99	7%	7%
£105-£155.99	9%	9%
£156-£304.99	9%	10.45%
£305 +	£27.45	10.45%

Contracted out rates

These are for people who will get an approved occupational pension.

Weekly pay	Employee	Employer
£41-£66.99	2.85%	0.90%
£67-£102.99	4.85%	2.90%
£103-£155.99	6.85%	4.90%
£156-£304.99	6.85%	6.35%
£305 +	£20.89	10.45%

Class 1 contributions count for all benefits.

If you have more than one job get leaflet NP28. Basically all your earnings will be added together to assess how much you should pay.

If you are not sure if you are employed or self-employed see leaflet NI40.

● Class 2 Contributions

These are paid by the self-employed. *See* leaflet NI41. If your earnings after expenses for the year are less than a certain level (£2125 a year in 1987/8) you can get a certificate of exemption. If you think you may need one apply straight away because it can only be backdated for 13 weeks. The form is in leaflet NI27A.

Unless you have a certificate you must pay. There is a flat rate (£3.85 a week in 1987/8).

If you are both employed and self-employed you will have to pay both Class 1 and Class 2 contributions unless you qualify for a certificate of exemption, which would excuse you from Class 2 contributions.

These contributions entitle you to all benefits except **Unemployment Benefit.** There are special rules for share fishermen who *can* claim **Unemployment Benefit** (NI47).

● Class 3 Contributions

These are voluntary contributions. You do not have to pay them. They only count towards **Widows' Benefits,** and **Retirement Pensions.** You may be sent a formal notice of invitation to pay them if you have insufficient contributions in any year for it to count towards those benefits. Unless you have dependants, or have a bad contribution record because you have been abroad or in prison it is probably not worth paying. If you are nearing retirement age you can ask the **DHSS** to tell you what pension you are entitled to and then you will be able to decide if paying the extra contributions will be worthwhile.

You pay at a flat rate — £3.75 a week for 1987/8. *See* leaflet NI42.

● Class 4 Contributions

These are not really contributions at all. They don't entitle you to anything. They are just a tax on the self-employed.

You pay 6.3% of your profits between certain limits. In 1987/8 you have to pay on your profits between £4490 and £15340.

See leaflet NP18.

● Credits

Sometimes you get a credit without having to pay. This counts as one week's lower earnings level Class 1 or Class 3 contribution if you haven't already got 52 weeks' worth for that year. If you pay the married woman's stamp you can't normally get credits.

You normally get a Class 1 credit if you are signing as unemployed. If you are unemployed you will not get a credit for any week when you earn more than the lower earnings limit or you work for more than one day or more than eight hours during the week.

You get a Class 1 credit for any week when you are registered as incapable of work or receive **Invalid Care Allowance.**

You get Class 3 credits for the year in which you are 16 and for the next two years to protect your pension if you stay on at school. You also get Class 1 credits for the year you are 16 and the following year to help you qualify for **Unemployment Benefit.** You also get the same credit in the year you finish a full-time course of study.

If you do an MSC training course for less than a year you will get full Class 1 credits. *See* leaflet NI125.

There are special rules to help widows and divorced women when they rejoin the labour market.

See leaflet NI51 for widows and NI95 for divorced women.

Men over 60 get credits towards their pensions if they need them because they have retired early.

Home responsibility protection

If you stay at home during any year to look after a child or an invalid you are excused from paying contributions and that year does not count as part of your working life for pension purposes. If you are receiving **Child Benefit** or **Income Support** without having to sign on then you should not need to do anything to have this recorded. Otherwise you should contact your local **DHSS.** *See* leaflet NP27.

Contribution conditions for benefits

For the contribution conditions for **Unemployment** or **Sickness Benefit, Maternity Allowance,** and **Widow's Payment,** see the entries for those benefits.

The long-term benefits: **Retirement Pension, Widow's Pension** and **Widowed Mother's Allowance,** all share the same conditions:

● The person must have actually paid contributions in one tax year on at least 52 times that year's lower earnings level; and

● they must have paid or been credited with at least 52 minimum contributions for at least 90% of their working life. Your working life starts when you are 16 and ends the year before you reach pensionable age or die. If you are over 55 your working life starts either in 1948 or in the year you started paying contributions if it was before then.

This means that most people can afford to have five years in their life when they had no contributions, without their pension being affected. Obviously if you die before retirement age your working life will be shorter, so a man with a family needs to worry about his contribution record more. If you die before you are 26 you can only have one 'bad year' without a **Widow's Pension** being affected.

Earnings related component

If you get some long-term benefits you may also get what is called an 'additional component'. This is part of the State Earnings Related Pension Scheme. The Government has announced that it intends to make changes to the scheme, but they will not affect anyone retiring before the year 2000.

The benefits you can get this addition with are:

- **Invalidity Benefit**
- **Retirement Pensions** (some kinds)
- **Widowed Mother's Allowance**
- **Widow's Pension**

If you earn more than the lower earnings limit your National Insurance Contributions are paying for this addition. If you are in what is called a contracted out pension scheme you won't get this. You get an occupational pension instead.

WAKE UP ... YOU'VE BEEN ASLEEP FIVE YEARS...IT'S TIME YOU PAID SOME NATIONAL INSURANCE

How much additional component do you get?

You can ask the **DHSS** to give you an explanation of what pension you will get. This won't mean much unless you are near to retiring because the amount you get depends so much on inflation. The additional component is protected against inflation. The amounts you have paid in each year since 1978 are increased to take account of the inflation that has happened since then. You get 1.25% of the total value of your contributions added to your pension yearly for up to a maximum of 20 years' worth.

Example

Mr Barnett earned £4000 in 1978/9. If he retired in May 1987 the calculation would look like this:

earnings in 1978/9	4000
deduct lower earnings limit	− 886
amount that buys additional component	3114
multiplied by inflation from 1979 to 1987	x140.7%
are now worth	4381
annual amount (1.25% of that)	54.76
weekly additional component (divide by 52)	1.05

This is only the addition for one particular year. Mr Barnett would get an addition for each year since 1978 if he earned more than the lower earnings level in that year. So if his earnings had increased in line with inflation he would probably have a similar weekly additional component for each of the nine years from 1978 to 1987, making his total weekly addition about £19 on top of his basic pension.

For more explanation see **Retirement Pension.**
A widow can get two additional components, one on her own contributions and one on her late husband's.

Nationality   *see* **Immigrants**

Negligence   *see* **Compensation**

New Worker's Scheme   *see* **Unemployed**

NHS charges   *see* **Health Benefits**

No fixed abode   *see* **Homeless**

Non-contracted out   *see* **National Insurance**

Non-dependants

If there is anyone living with you apart from your **partner** and your dependent children then they may be expected to pay part of the costs of your house — the **rates** and either the **rent** or the mortgage interest. The amount depends on their age and whether they are working or on benefit.

Who is a non-dependant?

Anyone who 'resides' with you, apart from your **partner** and your dependent children. 'Residing with' you means sharing some part of your accommodation, apart from a bathroom, lavatory or hall. It could be a child who has left school, an elderly relation, a friend or a lodger. Someone visiting you who has a home of their own which they are going back to doesn't count as a non-dependant. Nor do **students** who are part of your family (except during the summer holidays). Children don't count as non-dependants until they are entitled to claim benefits in their own right, even if they have actually started work. Generally this is at the end of the school holidays after they leave school.

If you are **blind** or get **Attendance Allowance** then no deductions will be made from your benefit.

Subtenants are treated differently from non-dependants. A subtenant is a person who rents part of your house and lives in it separately from you and your family. **Boarders** are treated as non-dependants.

If you have a couple or a family living with you then they only count as one non-dependant.

How much is deducted from my benefit if I have non-dependants?

	Amount Deducted	
	Rent or mortgage	Rates
Full deduction	8.20	3.00

Anyone over 18 working more than 24 hours a week and earning more than £49.20, (gross) or who is a **boarder.**

Lower deduction	3.45	3.00

Any one over 18 who doesn't have to pay the full deduction. However people under 25 on **Income Support** only have to pay the deduction for **rates,** not for **rent.**

No deduction at all
● **Youth Training Scheme** if not a **boarder**
● Under 18
● A full time **student** during a period of study, if not a **boarder**
● A person whose normal home is elsewhere

If you are an **owner occupier** on **Income Support** then the amounts listed for **rent** or mortgage will be taken off what the **DHSS** gives you for housing costs.

Northern Ireland   *see* **Introduction**

Notice	*see* **Employed; Rent**
Notional resources	*see* **Capital**
Nursing home	*see* **Boarders**
Occupational Pension	*see* **Retired**
Old age	*see* **Retired**
Ombudsman	*see* **Advice**

One Parent Benefit

Main conditions

You must be entitled to **Child Benefit** for a child who is living with you. You must not be living with anyone as husband and wife. (*See* **Partner).**

If you are married you are entitled to One Parent Benefit after you have been separated for at least 13 weeks and the separation is likely to be permanent, or when you are legally divorced or separated, whichever is sooner.

You get the payment for the eldest child who is living with you.

Amount

£4.90 a week.

How paid

With **Child Benefit.**

How to claim

Get leaflet CH11 from your local **DHSS.**

Time limits

You should be able to get up to 12 months' arrears.

Taxable

No.

Means tested

No.

Contribution test

No.

Effects on other benefits

Does not count as income for **Family Credit,** but it does for **Income Support** and **Housing Benefit.**

You cannot get One Parent Benefit at the same time as **Guardian's Allowance** or an increase of **Retirement Pension, Widow's Benefit** or **Invalid Care Allowance** for the child. If you get a **dependant's** increase of any other benefit for the child it will be reduced by the amount of One Parent Benefit.

Who administers it
Child Benefit Centre, Washington, PO Box 1, Newcastle upon Tyne NE88 1AA. Tel. 091 416 6722.

Appeals
You can appeal to the Social Security Appeal Tribunal if your claim is unsuccessful.

How to find out more
Books: *Rights Guide to Non-Means-Tested Social Security Benefits.*

Leaflets: CH11

Organisations: National Council of One Parent Families (*see* **Single Parents**)

One parent family   *see* **Single Parents**

Orange badge   *see* **Disabled**

Organisations   *see* **Advice**

Orphans   *see* **Guardian's Allowance**

Out-patients   *see* **Hospital**

Overlapping

Overlapping means that you cannot have certain benefits at the same time. You get the one which is highest.

The main benefits which are affected are:

- **Unemployment Benefit**
- **Sickness Benefit**
- **Invalidity Pension**
- **Severe Disablement Allowance**
- **Maternity Allowance**

- **Invalid Care Allowance**
- **Widow's Payment**
- **Widowed Mother's Allowance**
- **Retirement Pension**

You cannot claim more than one of these at a time. The detailed rules are given for each individual benefit.

Overpayments

If you receive a payment of benefit which you are not entitled to and the **DHSS** or the council find out there are three things that can happen.

1. You may be able to keep the money because it was not your fault you were overpaid.
2. You may have to repay the money.
3. If you did something deliberately to get money you were not entitled to, and which you knew you were not entitled to, you may be charged with obtaining money by deception.

Do you have to repay the money?
The rules vary for different benefits.

Housing Benefit
For **Housing Benefit** the council can recover any overpaid benefit unless it was 'caused by an official error where the claimant or a person acting on his behalf or any other person to whom the payment is made could not reasonably have been expected to realise it was an overpayment' when it was received.

This means that you must be very sure that you report *to the council* anything which might affect your **Housing Benefit,** in particular the fact that your **Income Support** has stopped. It is always best to notify the council in writing, and to keep a copy. You should not assume that because you have told the **DHSS** something that they will pass on information to the council.

The council is not obliged to recover any overpayments. If you feel that you have acted blamelessly, or that their decision is unfair, or that recovery will cause undue hardship, you should **appeal** to the Housing Benefit Review Board.

The amount which the council recovers should be the amount of the overpayment after deducting what you should have been paid. They will normally recover the overpayment by deducting it at a weekly rate from your future benefit, but they can sue you in the courts for it. They cannot just put you into rent or rate arrears. They can recover money from your estate after your death.

Social Security Benefits

If you have been overpaid the **DHSS** will probably write and ask you if you would like to repay. They can make you repay (by deducting money out of your benefit every week) if:

● you failed to disclose a material fact, or
● you misrepresented a fact

and, as a result, you were paid too much benefit.

You cannot 'fail to disclose' something that you did not know. You do not have to disclose facts in writing, but if you claim to have told the **DHSS** something by telephone and they have no record of it you may have a difficult job to convince people that you did tell them. Your duty to disclose information does not stop when you report a fact. If you inform the **DHSS** that your pension has gone up, but your benefit remains the same you have a duty to tell them again if it is obvious that the message has not got through.

Misrepresentation can be completely innocent. If you sign a statement that your savings are £2900 but in fact they have increased by the addition of £200 interest without your knowledge that would be misrepresentation.

Appeals

The law on overpayments is very complicated. The **DHSS** very often make mistakes both in deciding whether you have to repay benefits and in the amount you have to repay. You should get **advice** if you are told you have to repay money, and **appeal** if you think there is any possibility the **DHSS** have got it wrong. If you appeal the **DHSS** should not take any money back from your benefit until the appeal is heard. Do not repay any money in the meantime, because if the tribunal decides you were in the right the **DHSS** will not give it back to you.

How you have to pay money back

If you have to repay money it will usually be stopped from your weekly benefit. If you are on **Income Support** £4.50 a week will be deducted unless you have been found guilty of fraud, in which case it will be £6.30 a week. If it will cause you great hardship to repay the money you can ask your MP to write to the Minister, who can decide not to recover an overpayment in any particular case.

Sometimes the **DHSS** discovers an overpayment of benefit after the death of a claimant. They then have the power to recover the money from the estate.

Fraud

The **DHSS** do not normally prosecute cases of fraud unless they are certain they will win and more than £200 is involved. If you are found guilty of fraud you may be ordered by the court to repay the money to the **DHSS**. If you are accused of fraud you should get a solicitor.

If they suspect you of fraud they can suspend your benefit. They will usually ask you to come and be interviewed 'in connection with your entitlement to benefit'. If this happens to you get **advice.** *Do not go for an interview on your own.* You are entitled to have an adviser or a solicitor present. If your adviser cannot come at the time fixed you can arrange a new time.

If your benefit is suspended or stopped you can do three things:

1. Make a fresh claim for benefit. Even if you were not entitled in the past you may be now.
2. You can **appeal.** It will take at least six weeks before your appeal is heard.
3. You can claim benefit as an **emergency.**

Overseas student   *see* **Immigrants**

Owner Occupiers

Owner occupiers are entitled to help in paying their **rates** through **Housing Benefit** and **Disabled Rate Relief.** You can get help with the cost of mortgage interest. If you own your home jointly with someone who is not a member of your household you will get help with your share of these costs.

You may be able to get an Improvement Grant from your local council. If your home needs minor structural repair or redecoration you might be able to get help from the **Social Fund,** especially if you are old or mentally or physically sick or **disabled.**

Insulation

Tenants, owners and landlords can all apply for a loft insulation grant. You get 66% of the cost of the materials you need, up to a maximum of £69. Pensioners, or people getting **Mobility** or **Attendance Allowance,** can get 90% up to a maximum of £95 if they are also getting **Income Support** or **Housing Benefit.** If you get **Housing Benefit** or **Family Credit** you can get help from a local energy project if there is one in your area. The project will provide the labour, and materials worth up to £50.

What work has to be done?

To get the grant you must agree to have your loft, your hot water cylinder, and any pipes or water tanks in the loft, insulated.

How do I find out more?

Get in touch with your local council.

Improvement Grants

The Goverment have been considering changes in the system of Home Improvement Grants for some time, but no announcement had been made when this book was written. Consult your local council for up to date information.

Intermediate Grants

If your house does not have an inside toilet or a bathroom you are entitled to a grant of 75% of the cost of putting one in. If you are poor the council can increase the grant to 90%.

Improvement Grants

Your council may give you a grant if your house is old and needs repairing, but this is descretionary. That means it is up to each individual council to decide what help it will give. You might have to wait in a long queue, even if they do agree to help you.

Adaptations for disabled people

If the Social Services Department agrees that you need some adaptation in your home because you are **disabled** then they must provide it. They are entitled to recover their charges for doing the work if you are able to pay. They should not say 'We will not do the work unless you pay'.

For more details see the *Disability Rights Handbook*.

Income Tax and mortgages

If you are liable to pay **Income Tax,** which almost all residents of the UK are, then you will benefit from Mortgage Interest Relief At Source (MIRAS) if your mortgage is less than £30,000. This means that the Government will pay to your mortgage account the amount of tax that you paid on the interest for the year. Basic rate taxpayers receive 27% of the interest for the year. If you pay tax at a higher rate you can receive up to 60% of the interest.

Income Support and housing costs

If you claim **Income Support** any interest you have to pay on a mortgage is taken into account in calculating you much you need to live on each week. This is just part of your housing costs. You can only get help with the cost of a home if you normally occupy it, and with only one home. You are treated as normally occupying your home even if you do not at present live in it if:

1. you are a student or on a training course and so you have to have two homes (*see also* **students**)
2. you have had to move out of your normal home so it can be repaired
3. you had to make payments before you moved in, and you claimed **Income Support** before you moved in, and either
    (a) the house had to be adapted because of the disability of a member of your family, or
    (b) you were waiting for a **Social Fund** payment, and either you have a child under 5 or you are entitled to a premium for age or disability, or
    (c) you were in **hospital** or a home

You are still treated as occupying your home if you are temporarily away and intend to come back so long as you don't let or sublet it, you haven't been away for more than a year and you are not likely to be away more than a year. If you are in **hospital** or a similar situation you have to show that you are not likely to be away much more than a year, but in any case your housing costs will stop when you have actually been away for a year.

There are three situations in which you can get help with two homes if you are on **Income Support:**

1. You left your home through fear of violence, either in the home or from a former member of your family.
2. Either you or your **partner** is a **student** or on a training course and because of that you have to live apart.
3. You have moved and have to pay for two homes at once. This **overlapping** payment cannot last for more than four weeks.

If you are on **Income Support** you can also get help with:

● interest on loans taken out for repairs or improvements (if you have more than £500 **capital** you are expected to use it to reduce the loan)
● service charges in flats (with rules similar to those for **Housing Benefit)**
● payments you make under a co-ownership scheme
● rent you pay if you are a crofter or a crown tenant
● ground rent
● payments for a tent or the site, if you live in a tent

This list does not include all the items which were covered by Supplementary Benefit. If you were getting that in the week of 11th April 1988 you may benefit from **Transitional Protection.**

What loans can you get help with?

You can normally only get help with the cost of a loan taken out to buy or improve your home, or of a loan to replace such a loan. Interest on business loans secured on the home do not qualify for any help, unless they were taken out by your **partner** who has since left you. If your mortgage was partly for business purposes, such as a flat above a shop, or to pay your **debts,** you will only get help with the part of the loan which was to buy your home. If you are a sitting tenant and you buy your home while you are on benefit, the help you get with your mortgage will be limited to the amount of **rent** you were paying before you bought your home, unless there is a major change in your family circumstances.

It does not matter if the mortgage or loan is not in your name so long as the person who is liable is not paying and you have to pay in order to live in the home.

Limitations on the help you get

If you and your **partner,** if any, are under 60 you will only get help with half your mortgage interest for the first 16 weeks of your claim. After that you will get all your interest, and interest on the arrears accrued because of this rule for the first 16 weeks. Even if you stop getting benefit you won't have to suffer the 16 week restriction again unless you are off benefit for at least eight weeks.

If you have an endowment mortgage you will not get any help with the life assurance premium you have to pay. You should consider switching to an ordinary repayment mortgage if you think you may benefit for any length of time.

What to do if you cannot get Income Support when you first claim

If the only reason you didn't get **Income Support** when you first claimed is that only half your mortgage interest is counted, then there is a special rule to help you to get your benefit. If you claim again between 16 and 20 weeks after the first unsuccessful claim then for your later claim all your mortgage interest will be counted. There is no restriction on what you do in the intervening weeks. If you have an irregular pattern of work you should claim **Income Support** as often you can, even if you know that you won't get it because of the 16 week rule. That way you protect your right to benefit which you might need in four months time.

Excessive Housing Costs

If the **DHSS** think your housing costs are unreasonably high because your home is unnecessarily large, or in an unnecessarily expensive area, or because the running costs are unreasonably high, they can restrict the amount of help they will give you. Any part of your house which is sublet or occupied by **boarders** will be ignored for this purpose.

They should not restrict your housing costs if it is unreasonable to expect you to move, bearing in mind your family circumstances and the availability of suitable cheaper accommodation in the area. In any event there should be no restriction on this basis during the first six months of your claim if you could afford your mortgage when you took it on.

Subtenants

Normally if you have subtenants, any money they pay you will be taken off your **Housing Benefit** or your housing costs for **Income Support**. The first £4 a week is ignored, and another £6.70 a week if the subtenant's **rent** includes heating. However, any profit you make from subtenants will be ignored if you use it to pay off the **capital** you owe, or to pay any part of the interest which the **DHSS** will not pay. If you have **boarders** £35 of any profit you make from a boarder will be ignored anyway (although boarders are treated as **non-dependants**).

If you fall into arrears

Get **advice** as soon as you think you are heading for trouble. Don't wait until the bailiffs are knocking at the door. You are much less likely to lose you home if you tell your lender what is going on at an early stage.

The **DHSS** can pay your interest direct to the bank or building society, and if you have a bad payment record your lender will probably think that a very good idea. *See also* **Debts**.

Parents
see **Children**
Relatives

Parking
see **Disabled**

Partner

If you are married and living together, of if you are living as husband and wife with a person of the opposite sex, then you are a partner.

What benefits are affected if I have a partner?

Some benefits cannot be paid at all to a person who has a partner. They are:

- **One Parent Benefit**
- **Widow's Benefit**
- **War Widow's Pension**

There are special rules for some benefits to help **single parents**. If you have a partner you will lose those advantages.

How is Income Support affected?

If you have been claiming as a single person and it is decided that you are living with someone as husband and wife your benefit will be reassessed. The income and savings of your partner will be added to yours and you may no longer be entitled to any benefit.

What does living together as husband and wife mean?

This used to be known as the cohabitation rule. It can be quite tricky. There are six questions to consider. The **DHSS** should decide if you are cohabiting by considering all the six questions, and looking at your relationship as a whole.

1. Do you live in the same household?

This means that you live at the same address, you eat together and manage domestic jobs like washing, changing plugs and so on together. If you share the same pot of jam (assuming you both like jam) then you are probably living in the same household. It is quite possible for two people to live in the same house and not share the same household. It can quite often happen when a marriage is breaking up that the two partners lead quite separate lives at the same address, and, in that case, they should be able to claim benefit separately.

2. Is it a stable relationship?

A casual affair is not the same as a marriage. If you move in with someone the **DHSS** may not 'marry you off' immediately, particularly if you say that you are experimenting to see if your relationship works out.

3. What happens to the money?

If you share your money this is evidence that the relationship is like that of a husband and wife.

4. Is there sex?

Sex is an important part of living together as husband and wife. The **DHSS** are instructed not to ask you about sex, but you can volunteer information if you want.

If you do not have sex, and have no intention of doing so, then even if your relationship is very like a marriage in other ways you should not be treated as living together as husband and wife. If you have separate sleeping arrangements you should show them to the **DHSS** if they come round.

5. Are there children?

If you have children together then it will be hard for you to argue that you are not living together as husband and wife.

6. What do other people think?

If you go out together in public as a couple, that is evidence that you are a couple. So would the woman taking the man's name. But if you don't do these things then you can't necessarily show that you are not a couple.

If you don't agree with the **DHSS** if they say you are living together as husband and wife then you should **appeal.**

If you want to know more

There is an excellent piece in the *National Welfare Benefits Handbook*. The **DHSS** produce a leaflet, NI247 Living together as husband and wife.

Part-time course	*see* **Students**
Part-time work	*see* **Employed**
Patients	*see* **Hospital**
Pay slips	*see* **Employed**
Payment	*see* **Income**
Pensioners	*see* **Retired**

Personal injuries	*see* **Compensation**
Personal pension	*see* **Retired**
Physically disabled	*see* **Disabled**
Pneumoconiosis	*see* **Industrial Benefits**
Poisons	*see* **Industrial Benefits**
Pregnancy	*see* **Babies**
Premium	*see* **Income Support**
Premium Bonds	*see* **Capital**
Prescribed industrial diseases	*see* **Industrial Benefits**
Prescriptions	*see* **Health Benefits**

Prisoners

The problems facing prisoners can be divided into three phases:

- before sentence (if you are remanded in custody);
- during imprisonment;
- after release.

If you receive **War Pension** see that heading — the rules are quite different from other benefits.

1. Before sentence

If you are remanded on bail your benefits will not normally be affected. If you are remanded in custody you are still entitled to:

> **Sickness Benefit, Severe Disablement Allowance, Invalidity Pension, Maternity Allowance, Widow's Benefits, Retirement Pension, Mobility Allowance** and **Industrial Benefits**

unless at the end of the remand you get a sentence of imprisonment (including suspended imprisonment or youth custody). You don't actually get the benefit while you are on remand, you get the arrears at the end of the trial if you are entitled to them. If you have a family your **partner** will probably have to claim **Income Support** while you are on remand because the other benefits are stopped until the trial.

If you are on remand you can get **Income Support** to cover your housing costs if you are an **owner occupier**. **Housing Benefit** can also continue, so some of the cost of your home should be met, unless you are a **boarder**. You must tell the **DHSS** that you are in custody, otherwise they will assume that you don't want to claim any more, and stop your benefits.

If you have a family your **partner,** or a close relative (who may be a child over 16), may be able to claim **Income Support** as a **single parent.**

If a child **dependant** is remanded in custody any increase of benefit you are receiving for the child will stop. **Child Benefit** will continue for eight weeks.

2. After sentence

You cannot get help from the **DHSS** for the cost of going to court, or coming home, unless you are stranded and claim as an **emergency.**

The only benefits you can claim while you are in prison are **Child Benefit, Housing Benefit, One-Parent Benefit** and **Guardian's Allowance.** If you or your **partner** were getting **Family Credit** before sentence it will continue if there is someone who can cash the orders. While you are in prison you will not be credited with any **National Insurance** Contributions.

If you are looking after the child of a prisoner and the child has no other parent you may be entitled to **Guardian's Allowance.**

Housing costs for single prisoners

You can claim **Housing Benefit** to pay for your rent and rates while you are in prison, if the council accept that you are temporarily absent from your home. 'Temporarily absent' means you have not been away more than 52 weeks, you are likely to return and you are not likely to be away more than 15 months. In practice this means that if you are sentenced to more than two years you will not be able to claim any help with the rent or rates while you are inside. In any case you will not get any help with your water rates.

Wives (or husbands) of prisoners

For **Family Credit** you will not be treated as a **single parent** while your husband is temporarily away in prison. As far as **Income Support** and **Housing Benefit** go you are treated as a **single parent.** You should be able to get help with the rent or mortgage even if you are not officially the tenant or owner.

Visits to prison are paid by the **DHSS** as agents of the Home Office. If you are on **Income Support** or you are on a low income and you are named on a prisoner's visiting order you will normally get your return fare paid, including meals and overnight costs if necessary.

If you are on **Income Support** and your **partner** comes out of prison on home leave you should tell the **DHSS** in advance. Your money should be increased to cover the extra person in the house.

3. After release

You may be able to get a Community Care Grant for setting up home if you are old or **disabled,** an alcoholic or drug-user, or a young person who cannot live with your parents. *See* **Social Fund.**

If you are given pre-release leave and the person whose home you go to is on **Income Support** then they can apply for a Community Care Grant for the money it costs to keep you.

How to find out more

Probation officers should be able to help both prisoners and their relatives with their social security problems.

Private tenants

see **Housing Benefit**
Rent

Probation

see **Advice**

Quarterly signing

see **Unemployed**

Rates

Rates are a tax on property which pays for part of the services provided by your local councils, and for the police, fire brigade and so on.

Every property is given a reateable value, which is based on what it could have been rented out for in 1973, the date of the last valuation. The rateable value is fixed by the District Valuer, who is employed by the Inland Revenue. If you want to get your rateable value changed you should approach them. You will probably need to show that there has been a significant change in the value of the property since the rateable value was fixed.

The various local authorities in your area are obliged to set a rate each year, based on what they plan to spend. The rate must be paid by the occupier of the property, so whether you own your home or rent it you will be paying the rate.

If you have some facility in your home which is for the benefit of a disabled person, such as an extra toilet, or a garage, you may be entitled to **Disabled Rate Relief.** If your income is low you may be entitled to **Housing Benefit,** but however poor you are you will have to pay 20% of the rates yourself. If you get **Income Support** it includes £1 a week for single people under 25 and £1.30 a week for everyone else, which is what the Government estimate to be 20% of the average rate bill.

The Government plans to abolish rates for homes and replace them with a community charge, or poll tax. The only people who will be excused from paying the community charge will be **children** who get **Child Benefit,** convicted prisoners, people whose only or main home is a home or **hospital,** and people who are severely mentally handicapped. There will be a rebate system, but even very poor people will have to pay at least 20% of the charge themselves.

The community charge will be introduced in Scotland in April 1989 and in most of England and Wales in April 1990. In Inner London the change will be spread over the four years from 1990 to 1994. There rates will continue but be phased out gradually over the period. It appears that the community charge will vary between £135 and £355 per head.

Reciprocal agreements   *see* **Abroad**

Redecoration   *see* **Social Fund**

Reduced Earnings Allowance   *see* **Industrial Benefits**

Redundancy Payments

Main conditions

You must be dismissed because of redundancy. It doesn't matter if you volunteer to go. You may be redundant because your work place is closing down, or because fewer employees of a particular kind are needed. You can still be redundant if someone moves into your job when you go, so long as there are fewer employees as a whole.

Amount

You get a number of weeks pay, depending on how long you have worked for the firm. You cannot count any more than 20 years' service.

For each year between the age of 41 and retirement age you count one and a half week's pay. For years between 22 and 40 count one week, and between 18 and 22 half a week. Years under the age of 18 don't count at all. Multiply this number by your average weekly pay over the previous 12 weeks. There is a maximum amount of pay which can be counted (£158 in 1987).

The most anyone can receive is 40 x £158 = £4750. To get that you would have to be a man over 60 who had been with the same firm for at least 20 years and earned at least £158 a week.

How paid
As a lump sum.

How to claim
Your employer should pay you when you are dismissed or soon after. If you are not paid you must claim in writing either to your employer or to the Industrial Tribunal within six months of the end of your job.

Age limits
If you are under 18 you do not qualify at all. If you are within a year of pensionable age your redundancy pay is reduced by one twelfth for each month past your 59th or 65th birthday.

Excluded groups

● people who have not worked for the same employer for at least 2 years for at least 16 hours a week, or 5 years for at least 8 hours a week
● people who are offered a suitable alternative job
● self employed people
● people who are past pensionable age
● some people on fixed-term contracts
● share fishermen
● registered dockworkers
● merchant seamen
● crown servants and Health Service employees.

Taxable
No.

Residence requirements
You are not entitled if you normally work abroad, unless you are recalled to this country before you are redundant.

Effect on other benefits
None directly. But *see* **Capital** for the effect of the cash on **means-tested** benefits.

Who administers it
Your employer. If your employer is insolvent the Department of Employment will pay you directly. This can be extremely slow.

Special tips
This is only the legal minimum. Some employers may agree to pay more.

Appeals
If you have any dispute about your entitlement to a payment or the amount of it you must complain to an Industrial Tribunal within six

months. You can get the form from the Jobcentre. You should get **advice** as well, but don't delay putting in your form.

How to find out more
Books: *Rights at Work,* Jeremy McMullen; *Sacked? Made Redundant?* NACAB 1981. Leaflets: Department of Employment Booklet 16. DHSS N1231 Made Redundant.

Law: The law on redundancy payments is mainly laid down in the Employment Protection (Consolidation) Act 1978, as amended.

Organisations: Trades unions are the best source of advice.

Refugees	*see* **Immigrants**
Registered rent	*see* **Rent**
Registered disabled	*see* **Disabled**
Rehabilitation	*see* **Disabled**

Relatives

For Social Security purposes *close relatives* are defined as: parent, child, step-parent, step-child, parent-in-law, daughter- or son-in-law, brother, sister, or a **partner** of any of these.
Relatives are close relatives, grandparents, grandchildren, uncles, aunts, nephews or nieces.

Relevant education	*see* **Students**
Remand	*see* **Prisoners**
Remunerative work	*see* **Employed** **Income Support**

Rent

If your income is low, or if your rent is high, you can get help from the local council to help you pay it. You can still get help if you are not getting any other benefit or if you are working full time. *See* **Housing Benefit**. If you are not on **Income Support** you may still have to pay a part of the rent yourself.

If you rent somewhere to live privately and you think your rent is high for what you get then you should consider getting your rent *registered*. You may be able to get a fair rent set by an independent rent officer. You might get the rent reduced. Fair rents will be abolished soon, but so long as you don't move you will have all the advantages of a fair rent once you have been registered.

This is the amount that the rent officer thinks is fair for the type of privately rented property that you live in.

The rent officer will take into account:

- the age and standard of your home, including the state of repair
- the amount and quality of any furniture which is the landlord's, but not any which is yours
- any services like gardening or cleaning which the landlord provides
- how close your home is to the shops and bus routes
- disadvantages like noisy roads or factories
- other fair rents in the area.

Any improvements that you have made yourself will not be included in the fair rent.

Why register your rent?

- Registered rents are usually lower than unregistered ones.
- Once the rent is registered the fair rent is the most the landlord can charge. If the landlord charges more you can get your money back.
- It costs nothing to make an application.
- Even if your rent is paid by the council at the moment it might be hard to afford to pay a high rent if you get a job.
- If part of your rent is paid by the council at the moment, the amount you have to pay would also be reduced if the rent is reduced.
- Once the rent is registered the landlord cannot increase it for two years.
- If your rent is high you may not be able to get **Housing Benefit** for all of it.

Who can apply for a fair rent?

You must be a protected tenant. Most people in private rented accommodation are protected tenants. Landlords often try to deceive people about their rights by giving them written agreements which are misleading.

The law about protected tenants is very complicated, so if you are not sure get **advice** before you do anything.

If you are in one of the following situations you are probably *not* a protected tenant:

- your landlord lives in the same house as you
- your rent includes the cost of meals. (They must be real meals, not just bags of groceries)
- you get personal services, like cleaning, washing or making the beds, which are worth more than 15% of the rent
- you pay your rent to a University or college where you are a student
- you signed an agreement called a Shorthold agreement
- you do not have any room which is just for you and your **partner,** or you and your friend if you share.

If you are on this list then don't apply for a fair rent until you have got **advice.**

How to apply

Find the address of the rent officer for your area in the phone book. Ask if the rent at your address is already registered. If it is, and you are paying more, get **advice.** If it isn't registered ask for an application form. The form is not difficult. You will have to say what you think a fair rent for your home would be. Put a low figure. If you have a tenancy agreement you should attach a copy. If the landlord provides furniture make a list of it.

The rent officer will send a copy of your form to the landlord and arrange to come and see your home. There may be a hearing as well as an inspection. If there is you should get **advice.**

Once a fair rent is registered

The landlord can only charge the fair rent plus general rates and water rates, and no more.

Both the landlord and you have the right to appeal to a Rent Assessment Committee. If there is an **appeal** you will need **advice.**

Harassment or threats of eviction?

Your landlord is breaking the law if he tries to make you leave because you have applied for rent registration, or tries to evict you against your will without applying to the County Court for a Possession Order. It is also illegal if the landlord tries to make your life difficult by bullying you or changing the locks or cutting off the electricity. See a solicitor if either of these things happens. If it happens during the night or at the weekend call the police.

Changes

The system of fair rent will soon be replaced by a new system of assured tenancies. The rents under that system will be much higher. If you already have a fair rent fixed you will keep that rent, and if you were a tenant at the same place before fair rents were abolished you can still apply for one, but if you move to a different tenancy you will no longer have the rights to a fair rent.

Rent officer	*see* **Rent**
Repairs to home	*see* **Owner Occupiers**
Representatives	*see* **Appeals**
Reserve	*see* **Income**
Residential care	*see* **Boarders**
Resources	*see* **Capital; Income**
Restart	*see* **Unemployed**
Retainer for accommodation	*see* **Housing Benefit Income**

Retired

By the time you approach retiring age it is far too late to do anything about your pension. Your standard of living for the rest of your life is decided between choices you made years before and decisions made now and in the future by the Government. Fortunately for pensioners there are a lot of them, and most governments are quite wary of doing anything to upset such a large group of voters with a common interest.

The main benefits when you have retired are **Retirement Pension** and occupational pension. The Government have embarked on a complicated programme of change which will affect both, but the effects should not be felt by people retiring before the year 1999. You can get a leaflet called 'Saving for Retirement: Pensions' from any DHSS office, which explains the plans.

If you are facing redundancy *see* **Redundancy Payments.**

Your health is not likely to improve as you get older. *See* **Disabled** if you have any long term health problems. Many pensioners do not claim benefits that they are entitled to because of their disabilities.

Occupational pensions

There are so many different sorts of occupational pension that there is little that can be said about them in general, except that a very small occupational pension, or one which is not protected against inflation, is not likely to be worth having, because it will stop you getting **means-tested** benefits. If you are able to take some or all of your pension as a lump sum then this might be to your advantage, particularly if you have a **partner** to support. Occupational pensions for **widows** and other dependants are often so low as to be worthless. The remains of your lump sum may be much more useful to your family if anything happens to you. Most schemes limit the amount of inflation-proofing to 5% a year. If inflation increases to more than 15% again they will quickly become valueless.

If you leave an occupational pension scheme you cannot get back your contributions if you have been in the scheme for more than two years, but you can take the value of your pension rights with you to your next job.

All occupational pension schemes must now give you the right to pay Additional Voluntary Contributions which will increase your final pension and qualify for tax relief. Your total payment into pension funds is not allowed to be more than 15% of your pay, and your total pension cannot be more than ⅔ of your final pay.

You can no longer be made to join a company pension scheme, although you should think carefully before deciding not to join. Most company pension schemes are good value for money.

Information about occupational pensions

If you are a member of an occupational pension scheme you have a right to information about it.

Some information should be given to you automatically:

- basic information about benefits due and how the contributions are calculated should be given to all new members
- the amount of benefit payable on retirement
- the options for the families of members who have died
- notices if a scheme is to be wound up.

Other information must be sent to you if you ask for it:

- where you can see and copy the rules of the scheme
- the amount of benefit you and your family are due
- the amount of capital you could take with you to another pension fund

- whether you are entitled to a refund of your contributions
- actuarial information about the scheme
- a copy of the annual report and accounts

Personal Pensions

Under the 1986 Social Security Act you are entitled to leave the State earnings related pension scheme (SERPS), or your occupational pension scheme and use the money to buy a personal pension. This does not mean that you can get your hands on the money. You are only allowed to use the money to buy a pension.

A personal pension scheme is basically a savings scheme. It is independent of your employer, so it is not affected if you change jobs. You pay regular contributions from your pay and the Government puts in part of your **National Insurance** Contributions. When you retire you use the money which has been saved and invested for you by the finance company to buy an annuity. Unlike most occupational pension schemes you are not guaranteed half your final salary, or indeed anything at all. The value of your annuity will depend on the value of your investment in the stock market, or wherever, and the current rates of interest on the day you retire. The annuity will have to allow for a pension at half rate for your widow or widower if you die.

The minimum rate of contribution to a personal pension is only 2%, so you may find that salesmen try to persuade you to invest your savings with them and leave your company scheme. This may leave you with more money to spend now, but you might regret it when you retire. Be very wary of companies who give you quotations showing that they expect to pay you a pension of £100,000 a year in the year 2020. There is no guarantee that you would be able to buy a loaf of bread for that much money so far into the future.

You should be very cautious about investing your pension fund. It is very difficult and expensive to move your pension fund if you change your mind, and the older you get the more difficult it will become. If you are a member of a good company or occupational pension scheme, such as the teacher's or local government scheme, you are very unlikely to do any better on your own.

Occupational pensions and Unemployment Benefit

If you are over 55 any occupational pension above £35 a week will be taken off your **Unemployment Benefit.**

Housing Benefit and Income Support for pensioners

Many pensioners are used to getting **Housing Benefit** for their rent and/or rates, but have been reluctant to apply for other benefits. The rules for **Housing Benefit** have now been brought into line with **Income Support,** so that, for example, they both have the same rule about **capital** and **income.** And for both you are entitled to a *Pensioner premium* if you are over 60. For a single person this is £10.65 a week, and for a couple £16.25 above the ordinary rate of **Income Support.** When you get to the age of 80 you get the *Higher pensioner premium* which is £13.05 for a single person, and £18.60 for a couple.

National Insurance Contributions for pensioners

If you are still working after you reach pensionable age you don't need to pay **National Insurance** Contributions, although your employer, if you have one, does.

Health Benefits for pensioners

Once you are over pensionable age you get free prescriptions, but you still have to pay for your teeth and glasses unless you get **Income Support** or your income is nearly that low. *See* **Health Benefits** and **Hospital.**

Income tax for pensioners

Most of the income you get when you retire is taxable, so you are unlikely to get a tax rebate just because you retire. You should tell your tax office before you retire so they can make sure that your tax is right. If you work at the same time you draw your pension you will probably find that you have to pay tax on all you earn, because your pension will use up the amount you can have tax-free. If you are on **Invalidity Benefit** just before your pension is due you can stay on it until you reach retirement age. It's usually worth it because **Invalidity Benefit** is not taxable.

There is a special tax allowance for people who are 65 or over whose incomes are less than a certain amount. It is called Age Allowance. You have to claim it from the tax office; they won't give it to you automatically. In 1987/8 the income level is £9,800. The amount is the same for a married couple or a single person. You can still get part of the allowance if your income is not much more than that. The age allowance in 1987/8 is £2960 for a single person and £4675 for a married man. If you are married you can get the allowance when either of you reaches 65. If you are over 80 the allowances are £3070 for a single person and £4845 for a couple.

If a wife has a pension based on her own contributions she will get a tax allowance of her own for it. If her pension is based on her husband's contributions it will be taxed as part of his income.

The Inland Revenue produces two helpful leaflets:

IR4 Income Tax and Pensioners

IR4A Income Tax Age Allowance

See also **Income Tax.**

How to find out more

Age Concern produce a useful small booklet: *Your Rights for Pensioners,* about 80p.

If you have trouble with an occupational pension the Occupational Pensions Advisory Service (OPAS) may be able to help you. You can contact them through the Citizens' Advice Bureau or direct at Room 327, Aviation House, 129 Kingsway, London WC2B 6NN.

Some large firms, and the Workers' Educational Association, run pre-retirement courses.

The DHSS produce a good general leaflet: FB6 Retiring?

Retirement Pension

Main conditions

You must be old enough and you or your husband must have paid enough **National Insurance** Contributions. If you are below retirement age you must have stopped work.

You will be treated as having stopped work if:

- you don't work or
- you don't normally earn more than £75 a week or
- the work you do is 'not inconsistent with retirement'.

Amount

Basic pensions:

On your own National Insurance	£41.15	(Category A)
On your spouse's National Insurance	£24.75	(Category B)
Non-contributory	£24.75	(Category C
or	£14.80	or D)

If you are over 80 you get an extra 25p a week.

As well as your basic pension you may be entitled to an additional pension which is earnings related. Details of how this is worked out are under **National Insurance.** The most you can get is £34.75 a week.

If you worked between 1961 and 5 April 1975 you also paid graduated contributions. Contributions were £7.50 for men and £9 for women. You are entitled to 5.39p a week for each contribution you paid. You can get your graduated pension even if you are not entitled to any ordinary pension.

How paid

By weekly order book, or direct credit transfer.

How to claim

Get a form from your local **DHSS.** They should send you a form automatically about four months before you reach pensionable age. If you don't get one ask for it. You should claim in advance because it takes time to sort out your contributions.

You must not only claim your pension but also give notice of your retirement.

Age limits
You can get a pension from pensionable age, which is 65 for a man and 60 for a woman. If you don't retire then your pension when you do retire will be increased by 1% for every seven weeks that you go on working. You can also come out of retirement and go back to work and increase your pension in the same way.

When you reach retirement age, which is 70 for a man and 65 for a woman, you get your pension whether or not you have retired.

There has been much debate about the different ages for men and women, but there is no immediate prospect of any change.

You are a man for pension purposes if you were born one. You cannot get your pension earlier by changing sex.

Time limits
You can get three months' arrears of pension if you do not claim in time. You can get up to twelve months' **backdating** if you can show good cause.

Taxable
Yes.

Residence requirements
None for Category A or B pensions.

Category D pensions are different. To get one you must have been resident in Great Britain for at least 10 of the last 20 years and be ordinarily resident here either on the day you were 80 or on the day you claimed your pension.

Means tested
No.

Earnings rule
Between pensionable age and retiring age your basic pension is reduced by 5p for each 10p of the first £4 of your earnings over £75 a week and by 5p for each 5p above that. Your graduated pension and your earnings related component, if you get any, are not affected. Nor is your **Christmas bonus.** Once you reach retirement age you can earn as much as you like without your pension being affected.

If your adult **dependant** earns more than £31.45 a week the increase for them will be reduced.

Contribution test

There are four different categories of retirement pension:

- Category A is paid on the basis of your own contributions.
- Category B is paid on the basis of your spouse's contributions.
- Category C is non-contributory. To get it you or your husband must have been over pensionable age in 1948. There are no details about it in this article.
- Category D is non-contributory. To claim it you must be over 80 and not entitled to any retirement pension which is worth more.

The test of contributions for Category A or B is:

- The person must have actually paid contributions in any one tax year on at least 52 times that year's lower earnings limit. That would be £2028 in 1987/8.
- They must also have paid or been credited with contributions on at least 52 times the lower earnings limit for 90% of the years of their working life. *See* **National Insurance Contributions** for how to work out the number of years.

A widow or widower who is getting **Invalidity Benefit** when reaching pensionable age may get a Category A pension without having to meet the contribution test. Otherwise you can only get a Category A pension if you personally pass the contribution test. There are special provisions to help some people pass the second part of the contribution test if their marriage ends before they get their pension.

A Category B pension for a married woman is the same as a dependant's addition. For a widow or a widower it is the same as a Category A pension.

If you do not fully meet the contribution conditions you may get a reduced pension, so long as you are entitled to at least 25% of the basic pension.

This is a simplified summary of the contribution rules.

Effect on other benefits

Retirement Pension counts in full for all **means-tested** benefits and **overlaps** with most other benefits.

Additions for dependants

A man who has retired and gets a Category A pension can get an addition for his wife of £23.75 a week no matter how old she is. You can claim an additional £8.40 a week for each dependant child. *See also* **Dependants.**

Effect of going abroad

You can get your pension while you are **abroad.** However it will be fixed at the rate it was when you left the country and you won't get any increases of pension while you are abroad unless you are inside the EEC.

Who administers it
The collection of contributions is organised by DHSS Central Pensions Branch, Newcastle upon Tyne, but you can approach your local **DHSS** with most questions you may have.

Special tips
If you are getting **Invalidity Benefit** when you reach pensionable age you can choose to continue getting that. It is usually slightly less money but it isn't taxable.

If you were getting Invalidity Allowance within 8 weeks of reaching retiring age you can carry on getting it, but it will be offset against any earnings related component or guaranteed minimum pension you get. *See* **National Insurance Contributions.**

How to find out more
Books: *Rights Guide to Non-Means-Tested Social Security Benefits, Ogus and Barendt; Your Rights for Pensioners*

Leaflets: FB6 Retiring?; NP32 Your Retirement Pension; NP32A Your Retirement Pension if you are widowed or divorced; NP32B Retirement Benefits for married women; NI184 Non-contributory Retirement Pension.

Organisations: Age Concern

Review Board	*see* **Housing Benefit**
Reviews	*see* **Appeals, Backdating**
Road Tax	*see* **Disabled**
Safety	*see* **Emergencies**
Savings	*see* **Capital**
School	*see* **Children, Education Benefits, Students**
School meals	*see* **Education Benefits**
Scotland	*see* **Introduction**
Scottish Highlands	*see* **Hospital**

Seasonal Work

If you are judged by the Unemployment Benefit Office to be a seasonal worker you will have to pass special tests to get **Unemployment Benefit** or **Income Support.** You are expected to save up the money you earn during the season so that you can live on it during the off-season. The rules are complicated and if you think you may be caught by them you should look them up. If you are treated as a seasonal worker and this causes you or your family hardship, you may be able to claim **Income Support** as an **emergency.**

Who is a seasonal worker?

Most seasonal workers are employed in agriculture or tourism, but the test is of the work you actually do, not what your job is called. You can become a seasonal worker without wanting to be one if the only work you can get is during the season.

You are a seasonal worker if, during the last three years, you have regularly worked during part of the year and you have had a break without work for at least seven weeks in each year.

Where to find out more

Books: *National Welfare Benefits Handbook,* and *Rights Guide to Non-Means-Tested Social Security Benefits.*

Leaflet: NI55 Unemployment Benefit for Seasonal Workers.

Self-certification   *see* **Sick**

Self-employed

Self-employed people face a number of difficulties in dealing with the social security system, particularly if they are not well off.

Who is self-employed?

You do not have a choice about whether or not you are self-employed. It is a question of fact. Many employers in recent years have tried to reduce their liabilities and costs by persuading their employees to become self-employed. Some of these arrangements are genuine, but others are fraudulent, and both employer and employee may find themselves in serious trouble if they conspire to defraud the Inland Revenue and the National Insurance Fund.

The law about who is self-employed and who isn't is tricky. You may need to get **advice** if you aren't sure. But these questions may help you to decide.

If you are *employed* you should be able to say '*yes*' to most, but not necessarily all, of these statements:

● You have to do your work yourself. You can't send someone else to do it.
● Your boss can tell you what to do, when to do it, and how to do it.
● Someone provides you with holiday pay, sick pay or a pension.
● You are paid by the hour, month, or day. You can get overtime pay.
● You have to work set hours, or so many hours a week.
● You have to work where your employer tells you to.

There are many employees who cannot answer yes to all of those. A self-employed person would answer '*no*' to most of them and '*yes*' to most of the following statements:

● You are responsible for how the business is run.
● You risk your own money in the business. If it loses money you have to stand the loss.
● You control what you do, whether you do it, how, when, and where you do it.
● You provide the equipment you need to do the work.
● You can hire other people to do your work.
● If the work is unsatisfactory you have to correct it at your own expense and in your own time.

Advantages and disadvantages

There are advantages in becoming self-employed. You don't have to pay tax as you go along. There are opportunities for evading (that's illegal) and avoiding (that's legal) tax. But there are disadvantages too. You are responsible for keeping accounts and paying your own **Income Tax** and **National Insurance** Contributions. You don't have any of the rights you would have if you were **employed.** If the work stops you won't get any **redundancy** money. And if you damage yourself, or someone else, you won't be protected unless you have paid for your own insurance.

Benefits for the self-employed

There is only one benefit which is specially for the self-employed: **Enterprise Allowance** is intended to help the unemployed to become self-employed.

If you work more than 24 hours a week you may be able to claim **Family Credit** if you have children. If you are **disabled** and your earning power is reduced you may be able to claim **Income Support** even though you are self-employed full-time.

However much you work you may be able to claim **Housing Benefit** to help to pay the **rent** and rates on your home.

If you are not working full-time you will not normally be able to claim **Unemployment Benefit** because you won't have paid the right sort of **National Insurance** Contributions. If you were **employed,** or **unemployed,** or **sick,** within the last three years you may find that you are still entitled to **Unemployment Benefit** because of your contributions then.

If you are self-employed for less than 30 hours a week you can claim the same benefits as a part-time worker. *See* **Employed** for more details.

If you are **sick** you can claim **Sickness Benefit,** but *not* **Statutory Sick Pay.**

If you are pregnant you can claim **Maternity Allowance** but *not* **Statutory Maternity Pay.**

Means-tested benefits

For **Income Support, Housing Benefit, Family Credit** and any other **means-tested** benefit you may be entitled to, the biggest difficulty you face, particularly if your business is quite new or not very profitable, is that it is hard to prove how much money you are making or how many hours a week you are working. You will need to produce some sort of accounts, even if they are not very professional, if you want to claim any **means-tested** benefits. If you leave everything to your accountant you may find that if you haven't the money to pay the accountant you haven't any accounts to show the **DHSS** either.

For the details of how your earnings are assessed *see* **Income.** The special provisions for the self-employed are:
- your income is taken to be your net profit
- no allowances are made for capital expenditure, depreciation, expanding the business, repayment of loans, earlier losses, or business entertainment
- allowance is made for the cost of replacing equipment or machinery and repairing existing business assets and for interest on business loans
- you cannot offset losses from one business against profits from another, or against other earnings
- if you were working for more than 24 hours a week as a self-employed person and have now stopped any earnings you still get from that work are disregarded.

See also **DHSS** leaflet NI 39 National Insurance and Contract of Service, NI 27A National Insurance for people with small earnings from self-employment, NI 41 National Insurance for self-employed people.

Sentence   *see* **Prisoners**

Separated	*see* **Single Parents**
Service charges	*see* **Housing Benefit** **Owner Occupiers**

Severe Disablement Allowance

Main conditions

- You must have been incapable of work for 28 weeks continuously *and*

- Either you were incapable of work since before your 20th birthday *or*

- You are assessed as at least 80% disabled and

- You are over 19 or have left ordinary full-time education.

80% disabled is the equivalent of having your whole arm or both feet missing. You are automatically treated as 80% disabled if you get **Mobility Allowance, Attendance Allowance** or their equivalents, or if you are registered **blind** or partially sighted or have received a **vaccine damage payment.**

This benefit is designed for people who cannot get other benefits for **sickness** because they have not paid enough contributions. Most claimants are either disabled from childhood, or married women.

Amount
£24.75 a week.

How paid
By weekly order book.

How to claim
There is a claim form in leaflet NI252. Send it to your local **DHSS** office.

Age limits
You must be over 16 and under pensionable age when you first claim.

Excluded groups
People in full-time education who are under 19. 'Full-time' means more than 21 hours a week, but any education which is unsuitable for a person of the same age without disability doesn't count.

So if you are doing an ordinary college course for 15 hours a week, together with a course in sign language and extra English and Maths because you are deaf, only the 15 hours of 'normal' education would be counted.

Time limits
You can apply once you have been incapable of work for 15 weeks. If you have been entitled to claim for more than a month before you did claim then *see* **Backdating.**

Taxable
No.

Residence requirements
You must be in Great Britain and have been here for at least 24 weeks in the last 28 weeks. You must also have lived here for at least 10 years in the last 20 years.

Means tested
No.

Earnings rule
The same as **Invalidity Benefit.**

Contribution test
None. This benefit is designed for people who haven't paid any contributions.

Effect on other benefits
You cannot get SDA if you are getting **Sickness, Invalidity, Widow's Benefit, Maternity Allowance, Retirement Pension, Invalid Care Allowance,** or a training allowance unless the amount you get on one of those benefits is less than the amount you would get on SDA.

SDA is counted in full for **Income Support** and all **means-tested** benefits.

Additions for dependants
You can claim £14.80 for an adult **dependant** and £8.40 for each child.

Effect of going into hospital
The same as **Invalidity Benefit.**

Effect of going abroad
Benefit normally continues during a temporary absence abroad.

Who administers it
Local **DHSS** office.

Special tips
Most claimants will need to claim **Income Support** as well.

How to find out more
Books: *Disability Rights Handbook*

Leaflets:
NI252 Severe Disablement Allowance
HB1 Help for handicapped people

Organisations:
If there is an organisation for people who suffer from the same condition as you do they will probably be the most helpful people to talk to.

Severe weather	*see* **Fuel**
Sex	*see* **Partner**
Shared owners	*see* **Owner Occupiers**
Sheltered employment	*see* **Disabled**
Short-time	*see* **Unemployed**

Sick

This article is about the benefits you can get if you are too sick to work. If you have an illness which affects you but does not prevent you from working, or one which has lasted more than six months, then *see* **Disabled**.

The benefits you can get depend on your circumstances when you became ill, how long you are ill, and whether your illness is caused by your work, or by war. On top of these benefits you may be able to get sick pay from your employer (or through private insurance), **Housing Benefit**, or **Income Support**.

- If you are **employed,** and you earn at least £41 a week, you should be entitled to **Statutory Sick Pay** (SSP) for the first 28 weeks of sickness. If you are still ill after that you should be able to claim **Invalidity Benefit**. If for some reason you can't get **SSP** you should be able to get **Sickness Benefit** if you have paid enough **National Insurance** Contributions. If you are sick because of an accident at work, or an illness which is caused by your job, then you can claim **Sickness Benefit** without any **National Insurance** Contributions and you may be able to claim **Industrial benefits.**

- If you are self-employed or unemployed then you can't claim **SSP,** but you may get **Sickness Benefit.** After six months you can transfer to **Invalidity Benefit.**

- If you are not entitled to **SSP** *or* **Sickness Benefit** (for example because you are a housewife or have come from **abroad**) the only benefit you can get for the first six months of sickness is **Income Support.** After that you may be entitled to **Severe Disablement Allowance.**
- If your illness is caused by a war injury you may be able to claim a **War Pension.**
- If your illness is caused by an accident or injury you may be able to claim **compensation** for your loss of earnings and for pain and suffering. If your injury is due to a violent crime, or trying to stop a crime or a criminal, you may be able to get **Criminal Injuries Compensation.**
- If you are already getting **Income Support** because you are **unemployed** it is a good idea to change over to being sick if there is any chance that your illness may last for more than a couple of weeks, because, in the long run, sick people get more benefit than unemployed people. If you only have a cold it may be more trouble than it's worth going sick for a fortnight, because changing from an unemployed claimant to a sick claimant causes havoc to your supply of giros.

You may also be entitled to claim **health benefits, legal aid,** and **hospital** fares.

Proving that you are incapable of work
For all these benefits you need to be able to show that you are incapable of work. Normally you will need a doctor's certificate, although employers often let you certify yourself for the first week of **SSP.** A doctor's certificate will be sufficient at first, but after a few months, depending what your illness is, your employer or the **DHSS** may start to make further investigations. You may be sent to the Regional Medical Service for an examination. If you don't go your benefit will be stopped. If the Regional Medical Officer thinks you are fit for work your own doctor will be told. He does not have to agree. If he carries on giving you medical certificates you will be sent for another examination. If this third doctor agrees that you are fit for work your benefit will be stopped. You will have to sign on as **unemployed** to get any more benefit, but you should **appeal** against the decision that you are fit for work. Carry on sending in medical certificates, and get **advice.**

You are automatically treated as incapable of work if you are under observation as a possible carrier or contact of an infectious disease and you do not do any work.

See also NI253 Ill and Unable to Work, and FB28 Sick or Disabled.

Sickness Benefit

Main conditions
  You must be incapable of work for more than three days and *not* entitled to **Statutory Sick Pay** and either have paid enough **National Insurance** Contributions or be suffering from an industrial injury or disease (*see* **Industrial Benefits**).

Amount
  £31.30 a week (£39.45 over pension age).

How paid
  By weekly or fortnightly giro.

How to claim
  If you are **employed** but your employer doesn't think you are entitled to **SSP,** or your **SSP** has run out, you should be given a form to send to the **DHSS** with your medical certificate if you have one.
  If you are not employed you don't need a medical certificate from the doctor for the first week. You fill in a claim form SC1 from the **DHSS**, or the doctor's, or a hospital.
  When your medical certificate runs out you need to send in a repeat certificate within 10 days of the end of the last one, otherwise you will lose money.

Age limits
  You can still claim if you are over pensionable age and have not retired.

Time limits
  The first time you *ever* claim you have a month to get your claim in. After that you should claim within six days.

Taxable
  No.

Means tested
  No.

Earnings rule
  The same as **Invalidity Benefit,** but in practice you would be even less likely to get permission to do 'therapeutic work'.

Contribution test
  You must pass two tests:

1. In any one tax year you must have paid **National Insurance** Contributions on 25 times the lower earnings limit for that year.

2. In each of the two tax years which ended the April before the start of the calendar year when you make your first claim (that is 1985/7 if you claim any time in 1988) you must have paid or been credited with at least 50 Class 1 or Class 2 contributions.

Effect on other benfits
Overlaps with other contributory benefits. Counts in full as income for **means-tested** benefits.

Additions for dependants
£19.40 for an adult **dependant.** £23.65 if claimant is over pensionable age. No addition for children.

Effect of going abroad
Benefit will stop unless you are going for medical treatment, or you have been incapable of work for at least six months.

Who administers it
Local **DHSS.**

Special tips
You may still be entitled to Sickness Benefit even if you cannot get other benefits. For example, a woman who stopped work to have a baby might have the right contributions to qualify for Sickness Benefit up to two years after the birth of the baby. A person who had run out of **Unemployment Benefit** but was still signing on every three months for credits would still be entitled to claim. And if you are **unemployed** it is probably to your advantage to switch to being **sick.**

Appeals
To the Social Security Appeal Tribunal.

How to find out more
Books:
Disability Rights Handbook
Rights Guide to Non-Means-Tested Social Security Benefits

Leaflets: NI16

Signing on   *see* **Unemployed**

Single Parents

Who is a single parent?

You are a single parent (also known as a lone parent or a one-parent family) if you are single, divorced, widowed, or separated and have a child living with you. The exact rules are not the same for all benefits, and you might find that you can be treated as a single parent for some benefits and not for others. For most benefits the rule is that:

- you have a child living with you who is under 16 or under 18 and still in full-time education, and
- you do not have a **partner.**

You do not have to be the parent of the child. Any relative or friend of the child may be treated as a single parent.

What benefits can single parents claim?

There is one benefit that only single parents can claim. It is called **One Parent Benefit** and it is only worth £4.90 a week.

There are special rules to let single parents claim other benefits more easily:

1. Single parents and Income Tax

For **Income Tax** you count as a single parent if you are unmarried, widowed, separated or divorced and you have a child living with you for all or part of the year. You are still treated as a single parent if you are living with someone to whom you are not married, even if you have children together. If you have two children you can be treated as two single parents and get two tax allowances. The child must be either under 16 or, if over 16, in full-time education or following a training course full-time for at least two years. If the child is not yours you can still qualify if the child is legally adopted before the age of 18 or if you maintain the child, who is under 18, at your own expense.

If you are a single parent you can claim an additional personal allowance against your **Income Tax** of £1370 (for 1987/8), which is equivalent to the married man's tax allowance. This means you can earn up to £72.98 a week before you have to pay tax. To get this you should write to your tax office. *See* **Income Tax.**

There are other tax allowances for **widows.**

If you receive maintenance you may have to pay tax on what you receive, unless it is paid 'voluntarily'. Voluntary maintenance is paid without a court order. You may be able to reduce the tax you have to pay by arranging for the maintenance to be paid direct to the child. If you want to do this get **advice.**

To find out more

Inland Revenue leaflets IR29 Income Tax and One-Parent Families and IR30 Income Tax Separation and Divorce.

Daily Mail Income Tax Guide. (See p.98).

2. Single parents and Family Credit

You can claim **Family Credit** if:

- you have at least one child under 16 or under 18 and still at school living with you, and
- you work at least 24 hours a week (employed or self-employed), and
- your total family income is low enough. Any maintenance you get will be counted in full as income.

See **Family Credit** for details of how much you will be entitled to. **One Parent Benefit** is ignored in the calculation.

3. Guardian's Allowance

If you are bringing up a child who has lost both parents, or whose only living parent is missing or serving a long prison sentence, or divorced and not liable to maintain the child, then *see* **Guardian's Allowance.**

4. Rent and rates for single parents

If you have rent or rates to pay you may be able to claim **Housing Benefit.** There is a special premium of £8.60 per week.

5. Education benefits, health benefits, hospital fares and legal aid

If your income is low you may be entitled to these benefits. There are no special rules for single parents.

6. Single parents and National Insurance Benefits

For many benefits you can claim an addition if you have a child. See **Dependants.**

7. Income Support for single parents

You cannot claim **Income Support** if you work more than 24 hours a week (unless you are **disabled**) or if you are under 16.

The special rules which apply to single parents who claim **Income Support** are these:

- You can earn more than other people before your earnings start to affect the amount of benefit you get. £15 a week of your income from work is ignored, compared with only £5 for most people.
- You get a special premium of £3.70 a week.
- You can get benefit without having to sign on for work.
- If you are a **student** single parent you can get **Income Support** during term-time and holidays.

Income Support and maintenance

Any maintenance you receive from a former partner or the father of your children will be deducted from your benefit in full except:

- occasional gifts of less than £250 in any period of 52 weeks
- payment of boarding school fees
- payments made to someone else on your behalf if it would be unreasonable to take them into account
- payments in kind
- property settlements
- inherited property

If you get a lump sum of maintenance it will be treated as income unless you get regular maintenance as well. If you get maintenance under a court order which is less than the benefit you receive you can have the order made over to the **DHSS.** If you do this it won't make any difference to you whether or not your maintenance is actually paid.

Under **Income Support** law a man is liable to support his wife until they are divorced, and his children while they are under 16. (A woman is also liable in the same way, but as most liable relatives are men I am ignoring women in this section. It's quite complicated enough already.) He is known as a 'liable relative', and there is a special section in the **DHSS** whose job is to get money back from liable relatives. They will ask you about your husband, or your child's father. You must tell them if you have received any money from him, but you do not have to tell them the name of your child's father if you are not married, and you do not have to tell them where your husband is if you have a good reason for not wanting to. If they know you have a liable relative they will approach him if he is not paying as much as they think he should be. They will expect a man to pay as much for a child each week as they allow in your benefit. If the liable relative is on benefit they will not expect him to pay anything.

They may suggest that you apply for a maintenance order (or for enforcement of an order) against a liable relative. You do not have to. If you do not apply to the court for an order the **DHSS** can apply. They can go to the court for an order even if you are divorced and have agreed a final settlement.

This is a very brief summary of the law on maintenance. You can find a lot more details in the *National Welfare Benefits Handbook*. From the point of view of a claimant it means that there is no point trying to get maintenance unless you are going to have enough money not to have to claim **Income Support.** You just make your former partner poorer without improving your standard of living at all. It also means that if you are planning to leave your partner and become a single parent you need to get **advice** before you go. When you first go to the **DHSS** to claim after you have left, which is when you may be feeling most vulnerable, you will be put under a lot of pressure. You should take someone with you whom you trust, and preferably someone who understands your rights. If you have left your partner then you are entitled to benefit if you haven't enough money to live on. You need to be able to prove that you really are separated, and while you are doing that the less you have to do with your former partner the better.

How to find out more
There is a good **DHSS** leaflet FB3 Help for One-Parent Families.

Books:

There are a number of books on the problems of single parents. Make sure anything you rely on is up-to-date. Two which should be reliable are: *Going it Alone. Rights and relationships breakdown. A guide for unmarried women* by Anne McNicholas. SHAC 1986, £2.50. *A Woman's Place. Rights and relationships breakdown. A guide for married women* by Anne McNicholas. SHAC 1986, £2.50.

Organisations
If you have a solicitor s/he ought to be able to advise you, particularly about the problems of maintenance. If s/he doesn't know anything about benefits and maintenance you should find a solicitor who does.

There is a well developed self-help organisation called Gingerbread, with branches in most towns. They are bound to have members who have come through the same problems that you are having. The head office is at 35 Wellington Street, London WC2E 7BN.

The National Council for One-Parent Families is a pressure group which produces a lot of useful booklets. Contact them at 255 Kentish Town Road, London NW5 2LX. There is also a Scottish Council for Single Parents in Scotland at 13 Gayfield Square, Edinburgh EH1 3NX.

SMP

see **Statutory Maternity Pay**

Social Fund

There are four different sorts of payment you might get from the Social Fund:

Maternity, Severe Weather and Funeral payments,
Budgetting loans,
Crisis loans,
Community Care grants.

The rules for each different payment are set out separately.

Savings
For all Social Fund grants and loans if your savings are more than £500 you will have to contribute the amount of the extra you have over £500.

1. Maternity, Severe Weather and Funeral Payments
If you meet the conditions you are entitled to these payments, and you **appeal** to the Social Security Appeal Tribunal if you are refused.

Because these payments are unlike other Social Fund payments they are dealt with separately. See **Babies, Fuel** or **Death** for the details.

2. Budgetting loans
To be eligible for a budget loan you must have been getting **Income Support** continuously for the last six months (one break of up to 14 days is allowed). You have no right to a budget loan. It is up to the staff in your local DHSS whether to give you a loan. If they decide not to help you, or if you are unhappy with their decision about whether or how it should be repaid you can appeal to the local management who will review the decision. There will not be a hearing, but you may be called in for an interview. There is a fixed budget for the year for each DHSS office which is divided into four-week periods; if it has already been spent when you apply you will get nothing. It would probably be better to apply at the beginning of the four-week budget period if you want to improve your chances of success.

What do you get?
You cannot get more than £1000 in loans altogether, or less than £30. The DHSS will work out how much you can pay back from your benefit. They will normally want it all paid back within a year and a half, or two years in exceptional cases. If you are so poor that you cannot pay a loan back then you will not get one.

If you are offered a loan you will be sent a form to sign to show that you understand the terms and that you will pay it back. You can ask for a different repayment rate, but otherwise you have two weeks to decide whether to accept. The loan may be paid to someone else, for example a shop or a builder, on your behalf.

How do I pay it back?

The DHSS will deduct money from your benefits to reclaim the loan. They can take money from any benefit except **Child Benefit, Housing Benefit, Attendance Allowance** or **Mobility Allowance.** If you have a partner they can recover money from your partner. If you stop claiming benefit they will want you to pay back and they can sue you if you don't.

If you have no other debts they will make you repay at a rate of 15% of your **Income Support** (excluding mortgage interest), but this can be increased to 25% for short periods if you have no other debts, or reduced to as low as 5% or less if you have other large debts. The most you can borrow is 78 times this weekly repayment.

If your circumstances change you can ask for more time to repay your loan.

What if I need another loan?

If you get another loan you won't have to start paying it back until the first one is paid off. Your total debt to the DHSS is not allowed to be more than 104 times your weekly repayment rate, or more than £1,000.

What can I get a loan for?

The DHSS have a list of things which have priority when allocating their money. The top priority is for things which affect your health or safety, or that of members of your family, and things without which you will suffer hardship.

High priority items are:

- essential furniture and household equipment
- bedclothes, if you don't have enough
- essential repairs and maintenance for **owner occupiers** who can't borrow the money elsewhere
- removal costs if a move to more suitable accommodation is essential
- charges for installing and reconnecting fuel meters
- non-mains **fuel**

Your circumstances may bring you into the higher priority category. A pensioner living alone might get a loan for a television, while someone else would be refused.

There is also a list of things you can't get a loan for. It includes:

- main fuel bills
- housing costs apart from rent in advance and the cost of such intermittent items as emptying a cess-pit
- any need outside the United Kingdom

- education or training needs
- school uniform or sports clothes
- travel to school
- school meals
- expenses to do with a court appearance
- repair to a council house
- home help or respite care
- medical needs
- work related expenses
- debts to government departments
- investments
- maternity or funeral expenses

How do I apply?

You must apply to your local **DHSS.** They will give you form SF300 to apply on. They should decide your claim within 28 days. If you are turned down you cannot apply again for the same thing for the next six months unless your circumstances have changed.

3. Crisis loans

See **Emergencies.**

4. Community Care Grants

You do not have to repay a Community Care Grant. It is intended to help people to re-establish themselves in the community or to maintain themselves there.

Who can apply for a Community Care Grant?

You must be getting **Income Support,** or be likely to get it within a week when you move out of a home or institution.

What can I get a grant for?

(a) Helping you, or a member of your family to come out of a home or institution into the community.
(b) Helping someone to stay in the community rather than go into care or a home.
(c) Easing exceptional pressures on you or your family. This means family breakdown, inadequate or unsuitable accommodation which means you have to move, or persistent disability or chronic sickness. It also includes short-term boarding fees for a child who is about to be adopted.
(d) Helping you with the cost of travel within the UK because of a domestic crisis or to visit someone who is ill or to move to suitable accommodation. (*See* **Hospital** and **Travelling Expenses** for more details of these.)

You are more likely to get a grant if you are old or **disabled,** mentally ill or handicapped, or chronically sick, or have a disabled child. If you fall into one of these categories you may be able to get a grant for bedding, installing a slot meter, a washing machine, furniture, or even clothing. If you are not in one of these categories you probably won't be able to get such a grant.

The staff are told to consider:

● the nature and urgency of your need
● the state of the office budget
● the possibility that you will get help from elsewhere

They then have to sort out all the applications in order of priority, taking into account your circumstances. Applications under (a) and (b) above will have the highest priority.

How do I apply?
You must apply in writing on Form SF300 to the DHSS. Your claim should be dealt with within 28 days.

How much will I get?
Apart from fares the minimum grant is £30. There are specific amounts set down for some general situations, although these limits are only suggested and could be exceeded:

● Setting up home: £500 for a single person, £750 for a couple, £220 for each child
● Clothing and footwear: £150
● Repairs to your home: £400

You cannot get a grant for anything on the following list

● fuel bills
● housing costs
● any need outside the United Kingdom
● education or training needs
● school uniform or sports clothes
● travel to school
● school meals
● expenses to do with a court appearance
● repair to a council house
● home help or respite care
● medical needs
● work related expenses
● debts to government departments
● investments

- anything to do with a telephone
- anything which the Council should pay for

Someone coming out of **hospital** etc can get a crisis loan for **rent** in advance (*see* **Emergencies**).

What if they refuse me a grant?
You have the same rights of **appeal** as someone refused a loan — appeal to the local management.

There is a Social Fund Inspector who is responsible for reviewing the management decisions about loans and grants, but you cannot see him. You can only write to him.

If you are refused a grant you cannot apply again for the same thing within 26 weeks, unless your circumstances have changed.

How to find out more
Leaflet SB16: A Guide to the Social Fund.

Social Security Appeal Tribunal
see **Appeals**

Social Security Commissioners
see **Appeals**

Social Services
see **Advice**

Solicitors
see **Advice; Legal Aid**

Special Hardship Allowance
see **Industrial Benefits**

Spectacles
see **Health Benefits**

Sponsorship
see **Immigrants**

SSP
see **Statutory Sick Pay**

Starting work
see **Work, looking for**

Statutory Maternity Pay

Main conditions

You must have been working for the same employer for six months continuously in the week 14 weeks before your baby is due. For the last eight weeks of that time you must have been earning, on average, at least £41 a week. (The lower earnings limit for **National Insurance** Contributions).

To get the higher rate of SMP you must have been working for the same employer for at least two years continuously if you work more than 16 hours a week. If you only work between 8 and 16 hours a week you have to have been working for the same employer continuously for at least five years.

You are not obliged to go back to work after the baby is born in order to qualify for SMP. *See* **Babies** for more details.

Amount

There are two levels.

The higher rate is 90% of your average weekly earnings. That is paid for the first six weeks for those who qualify for it.

The lower rate is £34.25 a week.

You get benefit for up to 18 weeks altogether. You must take 13 weeks starting 6 weeks before the baby is due, but you can have the other five weeks either before, or after, or some before and some after the baby is born. If you stop work after you should or go back earlier you will get less benefit.

How paid

You are paid by your employer. You will normally be paid in the same way as you are when you are working. If you get maternity pay in your job then the two will be combined together.

How to claim

You must give your employer notice that you intend to stop work because of pregnancy at least three weeks before you intend to stop.

You also have to give your employer evidence of the date the baby is due. The maternity certificate form Mat B1 is the best thing to use. The doctor or midwife will give it to you.

Excluded groups

If you normally work less than 8 hours a week then you aren't entitled. **Self-employed** women don't qualify.

If you are in legal custody when your claim starts then you won't qualify for a payment at all.

The scheme does not cover the armed forces or certain mariners.

If you have a stillbirth before the 28th week of pregnancy then you don't qualify for SMP. You might get **Statutory Sick Pay.**

Time limits
If you give your employer less than 21 days' notice without good reason he does not have to pay you.

Taxable
Yes.

Residence requirements
You must normally live in the European Community.

Means tested
No.

Earnings rule
If you do any work for an employer in any week before the baby is born you cannot get SMP from that employer for that week. You can qualify for SMP from more than one employer.

Your SMP will stop if you work for *any* employer after the baby is born.

If you worked on a self-employed basis during your period on SMP that would not affect your entitlement at all.

Effect on other benefits
Counts in full for all means-tested benefits.

You could get **Widow's Benefit** with SMP.

You cannot get **Statutory Sick Pay, Sickness Benefit, Unemployment Benefit** or **Invalid Care Allowance** at the same time as SMP, but you might get **Income Support** or **Housing Benefit,** or more of them than you did before, because your income will be lower. *See* **Babies.**

Additions for dependants
None.

Effect of going abroad
Benefit stops if you leave the EEC.

Who administers it
Your employer.

Appeals
If you disagree with your employer's decisions you can ask the Adjudication Officer at your local **DHSS** to give a ruling. If you disagree with that you can appeal to the Social Security Appeal Tribunal.

Special tips
If you don't get SMP your employer must give you your maternity cer-

tificate back and a form SMP 1. You should take them to the **DHSS** and claim **Maternity Allowance.**

How to find out more
Books: *Rights Guide to Non-Means-Tested Social Security Benefits*

Leaflets:
FB8 Babies and Benefits
N1257 Employer's Guide to Statutory Maternity Pay
NI17A Maternity Benefits
Department of Employment booklet no. 4: *Employment Rights for the Expectant Mother,* from your local Jobcentre or Unemployment Benefit Office.

Statutory Sick Pay

Main conditions
You must be employed and incapable of work for at least four days together.

Amount
If you normally earn £79.50 a week or more your SSP is £49.20 a week. If your average earnings are between £41 and £79.49 a week you get £34.25 a week. If your normal earnings are less than £41 a week you don't qualify for SSP.

How paid
In the same way as your wages or salary.

How to claim
Tell your employer that you are ill. Your employer must tell you in advance how he wants to be told. You cannot be made to tell him that you are ill in person, or before the end of your first day of illness, or on a printed form.

Age limits
You cannot get SSP if you are over pensionable age.

Excluded groups

- **Self-employed** people
- People on less than three months' contract
- People who earn less than £41 a week
- People who have claimed a benefit for sickness or pregnancy within the last eight weeks

- People who have used up their 28 weeks of SSP within the last eight weeks
- People who have not yet started their job
- People who are 'involved in a trade dispute' (*see* **Strikers**)
- **Prisoners**
- Women who get **Statutory Maternity Pay**

Time limits

If your claim is late by your employer's rules (and his rules fit in with the rules laid down by the **DHSS**) then you may lose your benefit, unless your employer accepts that you have good cause for **backdating**.

SSP lasts for a maximum of 28 weeks.

Taxable

Yes. You also have to pay **National Insurance** Contributions on it.

Residence requirements

If you are liable to pay **National Insurance** Contributions then you are entitled to SSP.

Earnings rule

If you had two jobs you might be unfit to do one of them but still available to do the other. For example a teacher might lose her voice and be unable to teach but still able to work collecting glasses in a pub. The earnings from another job would not affect your SSP.

Contribution test

None.

Effect on other benefits

SSP counts as income for **means-tested** benefits. The only contributory benefits you can get at the same time are **Widow's Benefits, Industrial Benefits** or **War Pensions.**

Additions for dependants

None.

Effect of going abroad

Benefit stops if you leave the European Community.

Who administers it

Your employer.

Appeals

If you have a dispute with your employer about SSP you can ask the **DHSS** to decide whether you are entitled. You can **appeal** against their decision to the Social Security Appeal Tribunal.

Special tips

If you do not have enough to live on you will have to claim **Income Support.** Some employers have their own sick pay schemes, and, if so, that will be more important to you than SSP.

How to find out more

Books:

Disability Rights Handbook

Rights Guide to Non-Means-Tested Social Security Benefits

Leaflets: NI 244

Organisations: Your trade union will be interested in the way your employer handles SSP

Stoppage of work   *see* **Strikers**

Strikers

If you are judged to be 'involved in a trade dispute' you are disqualified from **Unemployment Benefit** and **Income Support.** You will not be able to claim **Statutory Sick Pay** or **Statutory Maternity Pay** if there is a stoppage of work because of a trade dispute at your work place on the first day of your claim. If you have **dependants** you can claim a reduced rate of **Income Support** for them. You can only get help from the **Social Fund** as a crisis loan for a cooker, or a heater, or if you are affected by a disaster. You may be able to get a Community Care Grant for **travelling expenses** in certain circumstances.

Your rights to claim any other benefits are not affected.

Who is 'involved in a trade dispute?'

You are involved in a trade dispute if the answer to *all* these questions is yes:

● Is there a stoppage of work?
  A work to rule is not a stoppage until someone's work is stopped by it.
● Is the stoppage due to a trade dispute?
  The dispute need not be with your employer, or involve your union. If you are sacked and there is no possibility of your returning to work then the stoppage is not due to a dispute.
● Is the dispute happening at your place of employment?
  If you work in a large business you may be able to show that the stop-

page is at another place of employment if the departments are sufficiently independent.

- Did you first lose your employment because of the stoppage of work? You cannot escape disqualification by leaving work for no reason two days before the strike. Once you are caught you cannot escape even if you would have been unemployed for some other reason after the dispute started.
- Is the stoppage of work due to a trade dispute still going on? If the firm closes down you can escape disqualification.
- Are you participating in the dispute or do you have a direct interest in it? Refusal to cross a picket line is participating in a dispute. You have an interest in the dispute if you are likely to gain something from its result, even if your union is not involved.

The only way you can escape from the effects of 'participating in a trade dispute' is to get another job. Moving away from the place where you were employed in order to try to start in a new industry will not do, unless you can show not only that you are not participating in the strike, but also that you have no direct interest in it. That means you must not stand to gain any money from the outcome of the dispute.

If you are ill during a dispute you are not covered by the disqualification, but your claim to be ill will be looked at very closely. You may be entitled to **Sickness Benefit.**

If you have a **partner** who is not involved in the dispute it may be better for them to claim instead of you. For the rules on which partner can claim *see* **Women.**

How to find out more

If you are involved in a dispute then you should consult your trade union. They should be able to advise you about benefits. After all, that's what you pay your subs for. There is an enormous number of cases which have gone to **appeal** about this part of the social security system. If you are going to be on strike for any length of time you need to learn how to get the best out of it.

There is an excellent, if rather large, book called *The Strikers' Moneyguide,* by Alex Dunn, published by CAITS in 1985. It deals not only with benefits but also the other financial aspects of being on strike. It is now out-of-date, but there is a supplement which brings it up-to-date to 28 July 1986. Use it with the *National Welfare Benefits Handbook.*

Student Grant

Main conditions

A student must have a place on a designated course. These are chiefly first degrees or equivalent, and include teacher training courses.

Amount

Yearly figures: £2425 in London, £2050 elsewhere, £1630 if you live in the parental home. (There are lower rates for Scots students). There are various extras, for age, disability, studying longer than the standard academic year, in vacations or abroad and up to £768 Older Students' Allowance. If you do the Postgraduate Certificate in Maths, Physics or Craft Design and Technology you get an extra £1250 a year.

How paid

Normally termly in advance.

How to claim

In writing to the Local Education Authority within whose boundaries you are ordinarily resident on 30 June before the start of your course.

Age limits

None. Students who are over 25, orphaned, or who have been married or self supporting for at least three years are regarded as 'independent' and get more grant, without a parental contribution.

Excluded groups

You are not entitled to a grant if:

- you have had more than two years' advanced further education
- already
- your conduct is 'unfitting'
  you are getting financial support from elsewhere.

Time limits

Must claim by the end of the first term.

Taxable?

No.

Residence requirements

You must have been ordinarily resident in the British Islands for three years before the start of the course, and not mainly resident in order to receive full-time education. There are some exceptions to this requirement.

Means tested

It is the financial situation of your parents or spouse which normally matters. No parental contribution is expected for a student

- who is 25 before the beginning of the academic year, or
- who has been self-supporting for at least three years in total before the course, or
- who has been married for at least three years, or
- whose parents cannot be found or contacted, or
- who has been in care for the last three years.

A parent will not have to contribute if his or her earnings (as calculated by DES rules) are less than £9900. Step-parents' income is not counted.

Earnings rule

£491 a year of the student's own income is disregarded. A further £905 a year trust income is disregarded for orphans. Another £2000 a year is disregarded for scholarships.

Effect on other benefits

Complex. *See* **Students.**

Additions for dependants

Yes. Independent students get an addition for spouse and children. Other students with dependants are eligible for a Hardship Scheme administered by DHSS Students' Unit, Government Buildings, Warbreck Hill, Blackpool FY2 0XW.

Effect of going into hospital

None unless attendance at the course is affected. If you miss your course for 28 days for any reason you should notify your Local Education Authority, who can demand repayment of part of your grant.

Effect of going abroad

Extra grant is payable if study abroad is part of the course.

Who administers it

Local Education Authority.

Special Tips

If you want to change your course or repeat a year you must tell your LEA at once. You will have to enrol on your new course within 14 months. You are only entitled to three years grant, but most authorities will give you another year.

These are the rules for mandatory grants — those which the local authority must give you. If you are not entitled to one of these you may still get a grant, but it is up to their discretion.

How to find out more

Books: *National Union of Students Welfare Manual.* £10 from NUS.

Students

The main source of money for students is the **student grant,** but these are generally only given to students on degree courses or courses at degree level.

Postgraduate students have to fend for themselves, but for social security purposes you can sometimes arrange to be treated as unemployed if you are not actually following a course.

Students on 'non-advanced' courses may get a grant from their Local Education Authority (called a discretionary grant because both whether you get one and how much it is if you get it are entirely up to them) but these students are generally expected to look to their parents to support them.

Apart from special arrangements for some students in unusual situations described below, most students can only claim **Housing Benefit, Health Benefits, hospital** fares and **legal aid.** You cannot claim **Income Support** or **Unemployment Benefit** unless you can show that you are really unemployed and not a student. Most people under 18 cannot get **Income Support.**

There are special rules to stop 'students from abroad' from claiming benefits (*see* **Immigrants**).

It is much better not to be a student if you want to claim benefits, and if possible to arrange that your studies can be disregarded as being part-time, or that your **partner** is the claimant with you as a **dependant.**

The Government has announced that it is considering further changes to the present system, so it would be unwise to make long term plans on the assumption that the present arrangements will continue.

Income tax for students
Although students have no special exemption from income tax most student income, and in particular the grant, is not taxable, so most students don't pay any tax. Because of this it is a very good idea to arrange any parental contribution to a student as a Deed of Covenant, so that the parent can claim back income tax. The National Union of Students produce an excellent leaflet called 'Covenants for Students' which explains how this works, and the Inland Revenue produce a form, IR47 to do it with. *See* **Advice** for details of where to find out more.

If your covenant takes your income for the year over the level of the normal **student grant** if may affect your **Housing Benefit.** If you earn anything during the year it will be added to your covenant for tax purposes and you may start paying tax as a result.

Income Support for students
This section only describes the special rules which affect students. You

must also satisfy all the general conditions described under **Income Support.**

The main rules that stop students from claiming **Income Support** are:

● Full-time students cannot be 'available for work'. If you are ill and unable to study you might be entitled to benefit.

● You cannot get **Income Support** if your parents are entitled to get **Child Benefit** for you.

The way these rules affect you depends on your age:

● *Under 16*
You can never get **Income Support** in your own right.

● *16-18*
If you are not at school you will be expected to join a **Youth Training Scheme** and you will not be entitled to any **Income Support** unless you are ill, pregnant, a **single parent,** or caring for an elderly or sick **relative.** Your parents will be entitled to **Child Benefit** for you in the year you leave school, until you start your YTS.

Some students do not have to be available for work and so can get **Income Support** although they are in 'non-advanced full-time education'. These exceptional situations cover students who are:

    ● parents with a child living with them.

or ● so **disabled** that they are unlikely to get a job in the next 12 months.

or ● orphans who have no-one acting in the place of their parents.

or ● living away from their parents, or person acting as their parent, and are 'estranged' from them. To be estranged you must at least be living apart and independently.

or ● living apart from their parents who cannot maintain them for reasons beyond their control, such as illness, imprisonment, or absence from the country.

● *Students over 16 in advanced education or over 19 in 'non-advanced further education'*
These students cannot claim **Income Support** except during the long vacation, and not even then if the course is regarded by the college as continuing. There are exceptions for:

    ● **single parents**
    ● **disabled** students who are unlikely to find jobs

● *Students over pension age*
People over pensionable age don't have to sign on so your benefit is not affected by studying.

Part-time students

There are two hurdles to beat. If the college describes the course as full-time that will normally stop your claim unless you can produce good reasons why their description should not be accepted. If the college describes it as a part-time course you have to get under the '21-hour rule' unless the course is 'advanced' — that is above A level standard. For advanced courses you are usually treated as a full-time student.

The 21-hour rule

This only applies to people in 'non-advanced further education', or on courses which the MSC sponsors. The rule is that:

Either

for at least three months continuously before the start of the course you were getting **Income Support** or on a **YTS** scheme

or

during the six months before the start of the course you were getting **Income Support, Unemployment** or **Sickness Benefit** or were on a **YTS** for at least three months and working full-time for the remainder of the six months

and

you must be prepared to give up the course immediately if a suitable job comes up — or at least prepared to say you will. It's not likely to happen. The course must not exceed 21 hours per week, not counting private study or breaks.

Housing Benefit for students

This section just deals with the special rules which affect **Housing Benefit** for students. Apart from these students are paid on the same basis as everyone else.

Entitlement

Students from abroad who are admitted to the United Kingdom with the condition that you should not 'have recourse to public funds' are not supposed to claim **Housing Benefit.** Even if you succeed in making a claim this might give you problems if the Home Office finds out. *See* **Immigrants.**

Rent paid to the college you attend doesn't count for **Housing Benefit,** so students in Halls of Residence cannot claim unless you are staying in Hall for a period of the long vacation when you are not studying.

You cannot get **Housing Benefit** for any week of the long vacation when you are not living in your accommodation, unless you were living there before you went to college. This means that you cannot get help with the cost of a summer retainer.

If a couple separates so that one of you can go to college it is possible for both partners to make claims for **Housing Benefit.** Your joint income will be used in the calculation and you will suffer the rent deduction on each claim.

How much Housing Benefit?

A student who qualifies for **Income Support** can get **Housing Benefit** in the normal way.

For a student not getting **Income Support,** a student deduction of £13.60 a week (£17.70 in London) is made from the rent for all the weeks of the year which are covered by the **student grant.** This is usually every week except the long vacation. The fact that you may not get a grant at all makes no difference unless you started your course without a grant before September 1986.

When the local authority does the calculation of benefit it has to treat any student with a mandatory award as if you received a full grant, whether or not your parents pay a contribution. Any amount in the grant for college fees, equipment, disability, residential courses or a second home is disregarded. So is the amount of the student deduction. Students benefit from a £5 disregard from either their earnings or any covenant income.

Unemployment Benefit for students

Full-time students on advanced courses can only claim **Unemployment Benefit** during the long vacation.

National Insurance Contributions for students

You do not have to pay **National Insurance** while you are studying, but you can pay voluntarily (Class 3) for up to six years after you have finished studying. It is hard to believe that the pension scheme we now have will survive unchanged until present students retire. As most students get jobs which give them decent pensions it seems unlikely that you will suffer if you don't pay. Mature students or men who have dependants should pay because you will protect not only your own pensions but also the right of your dependants to **Widow's Benefit** and related benefits.

Leaflets

DHSS FB20 Leaving School? and FB23 Young people's guide to Social Security

Advice for Students

Universities, polytechnics and most larger colleges have a students' union which can give advice about any common student problem. Most of them would also help students from other colleges, or people who are thinking of becoming students. There might be a special welfare officer or advice service, either provided by the union or by the college. The services provided by the unions tend to be more professional. Most students unions are affiliated to the National Union of Students who produce an excellent Welfare Manual and give support to their local students' unions.

Subtenants	*see* **Housing Benefit, Owner Occupiers**
Supervision	*see* **Attendance Allowance**
Suspended from work	*see* **Unemployed**
Suspension of benefit	*see* **Overpayments**
Tariff income	*see* **Capital**
Tax	*see* **Income Tax**
Taxi fares	*see* **Disabled**
Teeth	*see* **Health Benefits**
Telephone	*see* **Social Fund**
Television	*see* **Social Fund**
Territorial Army	*see* **Income**
Therapeutic work	*see* **Invalidity Benefit**
Time limits	*see* **Backdating, Boarders**
Trade dispute	*see* **Strikers**
Training	*see* **Work, looking for**
Training Allowance	*see* **Work, looking for**
Training course	*see* **Work, looking for**

Transitional Protection

When there are major changes in the social security system they are usually introduced on the basis of *no cash losers*. This means that those who were getting the benefit which is abolished carry on getting the same money they were getting before the change. Usually the amount you get is not increased in line with inflation so the value of this protection declines over time. It is for this reason that there are still people getting Workmen's

Compensation Supplement, which was abolished in 1948, at a rate of £2 per week. It was a good deal more valuable in 1948.

There is Transitional Protection for people who were getting Supplementary Benefit on 10th April 1988 and are now entitled to **Income Support.** If the **Income Support** you are now entitled to is less than the Supplementary Benefit you were getting you will get a transitional addition until the **Income Support** you are entitled to exceeds the Supplementary Benefit you were getting. You should also get either £1 or £1.30 to compensate you for having to pay 20% of your **rates.** If you can show that you were entitled to Supplementary Benefit, or more Supplementary Benefit than you were paid, on that date, you may be able to get retrospective Transitional Protection. *See* **Backdating.**

There is also a special transitional addition for people who were getting money in their Supplementary Benefit of more than £10.00 a week for domestic assistance. This special payment will not be frozen, but will be uprated each year. Very few people will get it.

There is a scheme for protecting people who were getting Family Income Supplement and now get **Family Credit,** but generally **Family Credit** is paid at a much higher rate, so it won't be needed.

There is no Transitional Protection for **Housing Benefit** or Housing Benefit Supplement.

Travelling Expenses

There are a number of different ways of getting help with travelling expenses.

For details see:

- **Hospital** Fares,
- **Bus Passes,**
- **Disabled,**
- **Education Benefits** and
- **Work, looking for** (this includes the cost of going to work if you have just started).

For claiming the costs of visiting your local DHSS office *see* **DHSS.** For the cost of going to an appeal *see* **Appeals.**

In some circumstances you might get a grant for fares from the **Social Fund.** There is no entitlement to these payments, but Social Fund Officers are told to consider payments for:

- Visits to **hospital** (to visit relations and friends)
- Visits to close **relatives** who are critically ill
- Attending a funeral (*see* **Death**)
- Helping to cope with a domestic crisis (*see* **Children**)
- Visiting a child if a decision about custody of the child is pending
- Moving to more suitable accommodation.

For each of these payments, if you get them, you will get the cost of public transport, or the cost of the petrol if that is cheaper. You can only get the cost of a taxi if there is no public transport or you cannot use it because of your disability. If necessary you can get the cost of an overnight stay or the cost of an escort for a child or sick person.

Tribunals	*see* **Appeals**
Twenty-one hour rule	*see* **Students**
Unable to walk	*see* **Mobility Allowance**
Underpayment of benefit	*see* **Backdating**
Unemployability Supplement	*see* **Industrial Benefits**

Unemployed

There are three benefits you may be entitled to for your regular living expenses if you are unemployed.

- **Unemployment Benefit**
- **Housing Benefit**
- **Income Support**

You should also look at the articles on:

- **Disabled**
- **Redundancy Payments**
- **Legal Aid**
- **Health Benefits**
- **Hospital**
- **Education Benefits**
- **Work, looking for**

And *see* **Income Tax** in case you can get any tax back.

Being unemployed is the next worst thing to being a **student** if you are trying to claim benefits, so if either you or your **partner** are **sick** you might be better off.

If you are involved in a trade dispute this section is not for you. *See* **Strikers.**

What to do if you lose your job

Normally the first thing to do is to go and sign on as unemployed at the Unemployment Benefit Office. If you are under 18 you have to register at the careers office as well. If you are still being paid your wages by your firm, or you were paid in lieu of notice, you are not officially unemployed until your wages or notice come to an end. This is not the same as a **redundancy payment.** If you are on holiday you are not unemployed either. If you are not sure if you are unemployed you should go and claim anyway.

There is one situation when you might decide not to sign on straight away. If you are not going to get **Income Support** for some reason (perhaps because your **partner** has too much income, or because your **capital** is too high), then the day you start your claim for **Unemployment Benefit** is important. If you did not pay enough of the right sort of **National Insurance** Contributions from April 1985 to April 1987 (perhaps you were a **student,** or **self-employed**) then you will not get any **Unemployment Benefit** if you start your claim before the 3rd January 1989, so you should delay claiming until then.

If you have just left school and are under 18, from September 1988 you will be expected to go on a **YTS** rather than claim as an unemployed person.

If you have been **self-employed** you won't be able to claim **Unemploy-**

ment **Benefit** unless you were paying the right sort of **National Insurance** Contributions in the right years (*see above*).

Housing Benefit is not affected by any of these complications. You should claim it straight away.

Why did you leave your last job?

If you leave a job *voluntarily without a good reason,* or you are sacked because of *misconduct,* then you will be disqualified from **Unemployment Benefit** for up to six months for 'voluntary unemployment'. You will still be able to claim **Income Support,** but for that period your weekly **Income Support** will be reduced by £13.35 if you are over 25 or have a **partner,** or £10.40 between 18 and 24. You can get this reduction halved if someone you claim for is pregnant or seriously ill and your savings are less than £100. If you have a partner they may be able to claim **Income Support** instead of you, and so avoid this reduction. The other way of avoiding the reduction is to find another job, no matter how temporary or part-time, which can come to an end naturally. You might get a job for a day as a babysitter, for example, or set yourself up as a self-employed shoeshiner. When the temporary job ends there will be no question of disqualification or reduction of your benefit.

If there is any possibility of 'voluntary unemployment' your **Unemployment Benefit** will be suspended and your **Income Support** reduced until a decision is made. The Unemployment Benefit Office will write to your last employer. You will be shown a copy of your employer's reply and given an opportunity to comment. You should explain your case as fully as you can. Get **advice.** You should argue not only that you shouldn't be disqualified, but also that if you are disqualified it shouldn't be for the maximum 6 months. If you are disqualified and you don't think you should be then you should **appeal.**

The law on what counts as misconduct is very complicated. If you are taking a claim for unfair dismissal to an Industrial Tribunal (*see* **Employed**) although the tribunal is considering the same facts it may come to different conclusions from the Social Security Appeal Tribunal.

If you leave your job voluntarily you will be able to escape disqualification if:

● you were forced to resign instead of being sacked
● you were trying out a new job and you were quite unsuitable for it
● your partner moved to a different area
● you didn't have a proper home in the area where you were working

If you think you had a good reason for stopping work then you should **appeal** if you are disqualified.

If you normally don't work all year then you may be caught by the special rules for **seasonal workers.**

Are you available for work?

To get benefit as an unemployed person you must be available for work. If there is any question about your availability you may not get any benefit. In the past if there was a question about your availability you would be directed to go to an available job. Although that can still happen in theory it is now impractical in most areas because there are no jobs to send you to. Instead you will be given a form to fill in — *UB 671 Are you available for work?* If you do not fill it in you won't get any benefit. There are 12 questions on it. If you get the answers wrong you won't get any benefit. You may later be interviewed about the answers you give, so you should make a note of what you put.

Question 1: What are you doing to find work?

The wrong answer is 'nothing'. List anywhere you look for jobs — newspapers, the Jobcentre, factory noticeboards. If you apply for any jobs keep any refusals that you get. Make a list of any firms that you approach for work.

Question 2: What job do you normally do?

If you have never had a job then it is all right to say so.

Question 3: What job are you looking for?

The right answer is 'Any job I can do'. If you are too specific you may be accused of restricting the sort of work you will do.

Question 4: Are you willing to consider any other jobs?

There are two boxes to tick. Tick the 'yes' box. If you tick 'no' you are unlikely to get any benefit, no matter how good your reason.

Question 5: Can you start work today?

The right answer is 'Yes'. The only excuse you are permitted for answering 'no' is if you are doing good works, like being a part-time fireman. If you are working or studying part-time you are expected to be able to stop immediately you find a full-time job.

Question 6: Are you looking for full-time work?

The right answer is 'Yes'. In theory you could claim to be available for, only part of the week, but in practice it is much better to promise to abandon any part-time work or other commitments that you have, in the fairly secure knowledge that you will not be put to the test.

Question 7: How far are you able to travel to work?

The right answer is 'Daily travelling distance'. Even if you put down a long distance it may be used against you.

Question 8: Do you have any adults or children to care for during working hours? If 'Yes' can you make immediate arrangements for their care if you get a job?

If you have to answer 'Yes' then you must say that you can make immediate arrangements (within 24 hours). If you have **dependants** then you may be able to get some other benefit instead. *See* **Disabled** or **Single Parents.**

Question 9: What was your weekly wage or salary in your last job?

Enter the correct amount, and state clearly whether it was before or after deductions. If you worked part-time say how many hours you worked.

Question 10: What is the minimum weekly wage or salary you are willing to take?

The answer to question 10 should be less than the answer to question 9. You don't have to promise to work for nothing (yet), but the figure must not be so high that you are unlikely to get any work in your area.

Question 11: If the amount at 10 is more than you have put at 9, please say why.

This is a trick question. There is no right answer.

Question 12: Please give any other details which you think affect your availability for work.

This is another trick question. Anything you say may be used in evidence against you. You should only answer it if there is something affecting your availability which the Unemployment Benefit Office know about and which you need to explain away.

What should I do if my benefit is stopped?

You can **appeal** against any decision about your availability. The suggested answers to the questions are not based on the law, they are based on what the Unemployment Benefit Office will accept without question. Legally speaking you are allowed to put reasonable restrictions on what work you are looking for, and there are lots of cases about what restrictions are and aren't reasonable.

You can also claim again and fill in the form with the right answers. You are allowed to change your mind about any restrictions you put on yourself. You shouldn't be too blatant about it, or they may not believe you.

What about part-time or voluntary work?

You must tell the Unemployment Benefit Office if you do any work at all. Voluntary work will not affect your benefit unless you do so much of it that you would not have any time to look for paid work, or if it stopped you being available for work. However committed you might be to voluntary work you should say that you will give it up immediately (that means with 24 hours' notice) if you find a job.

If you work part-time you have to show that you are still available for work. You can do this in any one of three ways:

● There is a reasonable prospect of getting another part-time job to make up your hours to at least 24 a week

● The part-time work you are doing would not interfere with a full-time job.

● You would give up your part-time job for a full-time one.

Your **Unemployment Benefit** may be affected by the *Full-time normal rule* if you regularly work part-time.

There is a good leaflet which explains the rules for all the benefits very clearly: FB 26 Voluntary and Part-time Workers.

If you are thinking of giving up a part-time job you should start signing on before you give it up, even if you will not get any benefit at the moment, because that way when you stop you are simply reporting a change of circumstances and not becoming unemployed. Then you will not be accused of being voluntarily unemployed.

If you do work for no pay (or for less than the going rate which most people would expect to be paid) you can have your **Income Support** or **Housing Benefit** reduced, unless the person for whom you are working clearly cannot afford to pay. In practice you shouldn't have any trouble if you are doing the gardens of old ladies, baby-sitting for **single parents,** or helping **disabled** people.

Short-time working

If you are laid off you may be able to get benefits as an unemployed person if you can get within the rules of any of the benefits. You are allowed to place restrictions on your availability so that you can keep your existing job.

Holidays for the Unemployed

As a matter of custom you are allowed two weeks' holiday during the year, if you fill out a holiday form before you go. You have to promise to come back if a job is found for you, but there is no record of anyone being brought back from holiday for a job since 1946. You must give a telephone number and address where you can be reached. It doesn't matter what number you give. There won't be any messages. If you go and don't leave a number or address (say for a camping holiday) you won't get any benefit. If you say you are going **abroad** your benefit will stop. It should continue if you are within the European Community.

You can sign on at any Unemployment Benefit Office in the country, so long as you sign on your normal signing day. You are supposed to be actively seeking employment, and you can wander around the country looking for work. You can wander around Europe and sign on at various foreign Unemployment Benefit Offices. If you want to try this you must be careful that your **Income Support** isn't cut off because you are not living at your stated address.

Restart

Every unemployed person who has been out of work for more than six months is called into a Jobcentre for an interview under the Government's Restart programme. If you can't go to the interview you should tell the Jobcentre. They will arrange another time. If you don't go to the first interview you will be offered another one. If you don't turn up to this one without a good reason your benefit will be stopped.

If your benefit is stopped you should immediately tell the **DHSS** or Unemployment Benefit Office if you had a good reason for not going to either interview. You may get your benefit restored. You can volunteer to go to another interview. If you do your benefit will start again from the next payday after the interview. If you have no money to live on until then you can claim as an **emergency.** You can also **appeal** against the decision to stop your money.

Although you have to go to the interview none of the options you will be given at the interview is compulsory. You do not have to make a decision there and then. You can decide for yourself at home whether you want to try any of the options. If you refuse all of the options without considering them your benefit might be affected because your availability for work is doubtful.

Restart options:

● Jobclub. A group of 12 people are given two weeks in a Jobcentre with coaching in how to look for work, free telephones, stamps, envelopes and stationery. Very useful if you really want to look for a job, but there aren't many places on this option.

● Training. *See* **Work — looking for,** for details of the courses.

● Restart courses. A one week course at a college, showing how to look for jobs more effectively. This option is easier to get on than the others.

● Jobstart. *See* **Work — looking for.**

● **Community programme.**

● **Enterprise allowance.**

● Voluntary Projects Programme. Volunteer work with local charities.

● New Workers' Scheme. A £15 a week subsidy to an employer for taking on an 18 to 20-year-old on wages of less than £65 a week.

● A Real Job! This is the Big Prize. You are unlikely to get one out of Restart. Only about 1 in every hundred people get a job after a

Restart interview, about the same number who would have found a job anyway in that time. You may be sent for an interview, and it would be foolish to refuse to go, whatever the job.

Seasonal work

If you live in an area where there is short-term seasonal work your **Income Support** will be stopped for up to six weeks if you turn down a reasonable opportunity of short-term work. This only applies to people between the ages of 18 and 45 who have no children and are not pregnant.

See **Seasonal Work** for details of how your benefit will be affected if you do regular seasonal work.

Refusal to maintain yourself

If the **DHSS** think you are persistently avoiding work you can be sent to a re-establishment or training centre to restore your will to work. You can appeal against being sent if you think you haven't lost the will to work.

You can even be prosecuted for the offence of 'persistently refusing or neglecting to maintain yourself'. This is very rare.

Where to find out more
Books:
National Welfare Benefits Handbook
Rights Guide to Non-Means-Tested Social Security Benefits
The Unemployment Handbook, by Guy Dauncey

Leaflets:
There is a DHSS leaflet FB9 Unemployed, but it isn't very informative.

Organisations:
There are unemployed people's centres in many areas, mostly sponsored by the TUC and staffed by people on the **Community Programme.** They are very variable in what they can do for you.

The Unemployment Unit, 9 Poland Street, London W1V 3DG, is a very effective pressure group, and produces excellent leaflets and newsletters. They will be interested to hear about your experiences.

Warning. Be very cautious about asking the staff in Unemployment Benefit Offices for advice. They know very little about benefits, in general. They are only trained to carry out clerical tasks.

Unemployment Benefit

Main conditions
You must be unemployed and available for work on the day you claim. Benefit is not paid for the first three days of your claim.

Amount
£32.75 a week or £5.46 a day.

How paid
By giro fortnightly in arrears.

How to claim
Sign on at any Unemployment Benefit Office. They don't have areas. Once you are signed on you will have to sign every fortnight. You can be asked to sign on as often as they want you to. If you work part-time you will have to sign on weekly, but at any time that is convenient to you.

Age limits
If you are over pension age and not **retired** you get £41.15 a week.

Excluded groups
- **strikers**
- some **seasonal workers**
- people who are getting pay in lieu of notice or get **compensation** for unfair dismissal from an Industrial Tribunal (*see* **Employed**)
- people who are voluntarily unemployed (*see* **Unemployed**) for up to six months
- **students,** except during the long vacation.

Time limits
You will not get any benefit for days before you claim unless you can show good cause for **backdating** your late claim. You do not get benefit for the first three days of a period of interruption of employment.

How long does it last
312 days (benefit is not paid for Sundays). Once you have had your 312 days you must work for at least 13 weeks (not necessarily altogether) before you can qualify for benefit again. If you get a job before your benefit runs out you must work for eight weeks before you start a new period of interruption of employment and start a new period of 312 days entitlement.

Taxable
Yes — but no tax will be deducted from your benefit.

Residence requirements
You must be within the EEC.

Means tested
No — if you are under 55.

If you are 55 or over and receive an occupational pension of more than £35 a week your benefit will be reduced by 10p for each 10p that your pension exceeds £35. This does not apply to redundancy payments.

Earnings rule
If you earn more than £2 on a day you will not get benefit for that day. Benefit is not paid for Sundays.

If you are a part-time worker you need to show that you are still available for work (*see* **Unemployed**), and you may fall foul of the full-time normal rule:

If you normally only work on certain days of the week you cannot claim **Unemployment Benefit** for the other days (although you may be able to claim **Income Support**). The difficulty is deciding what is normal for you. It depends a lot on how long your pattern of work has been the same. A man who only worked for one hour a week as a pools' collector was caught by this rule because he had been doing the same thing for seven years.

Contribution test
In the last two tax years you must have actually paid at least 25 times the minimum weekly **National Insurance** Contributions Class 1, and you must have paid or been credited with 50 times the minimum weekly National Insurance Contributions Class 1 in each of the tax years that ended before the benefit year you are claiming in began. So if you claim any time in 1988 the contribution year is 1985/7.

There are special rules for share fishermen.

Effects on other benefits
Taken fully into account by all other benefits.

Additions for dependants
£20.20 for an adult. £24.75 if the claimant is over pensionable age. There are no additions for **children.**

Effect of going abroad
If you are within the EEC you should still be able to claim.

Who administers it
Your local Unemployment Benefit Office.

Special tips
Unemployment Benefit is not enough to live on. You will probably have to claim **Income Support** or **Housing Benefit** as well.

Appeals
You can **appeal** to the Social Security Appeal Tribunal about almost any decision affecting your benefit.

How to find out more
Books:
Rights Guide to Non-Means-Tested Social Security Benefits; Ogus and Barendt's The Law of Social Security.

Leaflets:
FB9 Unemployed?
NI12 Unemployment Benefit
NI230 Unemployment Benefit and your occupational pension

Organisations: Your trade union may be able to help you in arguments about entitlement to Unemployment Benefit.

Unfair dismissal   *see* **Employed**

Unmarried   *see* **Partner**

Urgent cases   *see* **Emergencies**

Vaccine Damage Payment

Main conditions
● You must be severely disabled as a result of vaccination. (It is not necessary for you to have been vaccinated).
● Your disablement must be assessed as at least 80%.
● The vaccination must have been for diptheria, tetanus, whooping cough, polio, measles, rubella, or TB.
● You must have been vaccinated before you were 18, or during an outbreak of the disease in the UK.

Amount
£20,000.

How to claim
On the application form in leaflet HB3.

Age limits

You must be at least 2 years old. If the person is now dead they must have lived to be at least 2.

Time limits

You must claim within 6 years of the vaccination or by the time you are 8 years old, if you were vaccinated before you were 2.

Taxable

No.

Effect on other benefits

Can be ignored as resource for **Income Support** if the money is held for a child.

Residence requirements

The vaccination must have been in the UK or the Isle of Man. Families of the armed forces, vaccinated by service medical facilities, can claim. You must normally live in the UK or the Isle of Man.

Who administers it

Vaccine Damage Payments Unit, DHSS, North Fylde Central Offices, Norcross, Blackpool, FY5 3TA.

Appeals

There is no right of **appeal,** but it would be possible to apply for judicial review of a decision.

How to find out more

Books: *Disability Rights Handbook.*

Leaflets: HB3 Payments for severe vaccine damage, from the unit in Blackpool.

Law: Vaccine Damage Payments Act 1979

Organisations: Association of Parents of Vaccine Damaged Children, c/o Mrs Rosemary Fox, 2 Church Street, Shipston on Stour, Warwickshire, CV36 4AP (enclose sae if you write to her).

Visiting hospital *see* **Hospital**

Visitors *see* **Immigrants**

Vitamins *see* **Health Benefits**

Voluntarily leaving work	*see* **Unemployed**
Voluntary contributions	*see* **National Insurance**
Voluntary unemployment	*see* **Unemployed**
Voluntary work	*see* **Employed** **Unemployed**
Wages	*see* **Income**
Wages Councils	*see* **Employed**

War Pensions

War Disablement Pension

Main conditions
You qualify if any of these things apply to you:

- You were injured or disabled because of service in the forces in the 1914-18 war or anytime since 2 September 1939.
- You were disabled as a result of the 1939-45 war.
- You were a merchant seaman and were injured in war.

You can also qualify if you have an injury, not a result of your service, which is made worse by service.

Amount
Rate for 100% disablement is £67.20 a week for privates or £3504 a year for officers. The amount you get depends on how disabled you are. There is a very small addition for rank, which has not been increased since 1964. For example a corporal who is 20% disabled gets 4 pence a week more than a private who is 20% disabled.

How paid
If your disablement is assessed at less than 20% you will get a single payment. If it is 20% or more you will get a pension. So an officer who loses a big toe gets £3210. A private's big toe is worth £30 less.

Officers are paid monthly or quarterly. Other ranks are paid weekly.

How to claim
Write to: War Pensions Branch, DHSS, Norcross, Blackpool, FY5 3TA.

They will need to know your full name and, if you were in the Forces, your service number, rank or rating, what regiment or corps you served in and your dates of enlistment and discharge. If you don't know all these things don't be put off. Claim anyway and tell them as much as you can.

If you are claiming for an injury although you weren't in the forces you will have to give as much information as you can about how you were injured or disabled.

If you are discharged from the forces because of your disability your claim will be considered automatically. You shouldn't have to do anything.

Excluded groups

You may not get a pension if your injury was caused by your own 'serious negligence or misconduct'. You may lose up to half your pension if you refuse medical treatment.

You cannot get a pension until you have left the service.

You may lose your pension if you are imprisoned, but payment may be made to your family while you are in prison. When you are released your pension will be restored and you may get up to a year's arrears.

Time limits

None. If you claim more than 7 years after you have left the service you will have to prove that you are eligible. Your claim can be backdated to the day you were invalided out of the service if that was not more than six months before.

Taxable

No.

Residence requirements

You may lose your pension if you are deported.

Means tested

No.

Earnings rule

None.

Contribution test

None.

Effect on other benefits

The first £5 is ignored for **Income Support** and **Housing Benefit.** War Disablement Pension does not affect any of the National Insurance contributory benefits but you cannot get an allowance for the same thing as an extra both to a War Pension and to an Industrial Disablement Benefit.

Additions for dependants

You can get an addition for a wife, parent or husband (£1 a week), or a child (30p a week). If you are entitled to a similar addition to another benefit you will get the one which is higher.

Effect of going into hospital

If you go into hospital or cannot work because you are having treatment for your war disability you get a pension at the 100% rate for that week, even if you don't normally get a pension.

Effect of going abroad

Benefit continues.

Who administers it

War Pensions Office, Norcross, Blackpool, FY5 3TA. Tel. 0253 856123.

Special tips

There is a wide range of extra benefits available for war pensioners, similar to the benefits for Industrial Injuries. There is also a special welfare services for war pensioners.

Death

If a war pensioner dies from his war disablement relatives can make their own arrangements for the funeral and claim back the basic costs from the **DHSS** so long as they claim within three months of the funeral.

How to find out more

Leaflets:

FB16 Sick or Injured Through Service in the Armed Forces
MPL154 Rates of War Pensions and Allowances
MPL153 Help for the War Disabled
NI211A War Pensioners — Help with Transport
MPL120 War Pensioners and Widows going Abroad
NI50 National Insurance Guide for War Pensioners

War Widow's Pension

Main conditions

Your husband must have

- died as a result of service in the Armed Forces during the 1914-18 war or any time after 2.9.39 or
- been a civilian who died as a result of a war injury or war service injury in the 1939-45 war or
- been a merchant seaman whose death was because of a wound or disease received during the war or detention by the enemy or
- been getting a war pension constant attendance allowance when he died.

It is possible for a widower to get a pension if he is incapable of supporting himself.

Amount

£53.50 a week for a private's widow. Extra allowances of £5.75 when you are 65, £11.50 when you are 70 and £14.45 when you are 80. Lower rate of £12.35 payable to childless widows under 40 at the time of their husband's death if they are able to support themselves.

The widows of senior officers (Lt-Col and above) are always paid at the higher rate, no matter what their age or circumstances, because, presumably, they are not expected to go out to work.

If you were not married you can still get benefit if you are looking after his child and get **Child Benefit.**

How to claim

Write to: War Pensions Branch, DHSS, Norcross, Blackpool, FY5 3TA.

They will need to know not only your full name but also your late husband's full name and, if he had a War Pension, his war pension reference number.

Excluded groups

Benefit stops if you marry or cohabit. The widows of 'other ranks' may get 1 year's pension as a gratuity if this happens. Officer's widows don't get the gratuity but they may get their pension back if their new husband dies. You may lose the benefit if you are imprisoned.

Taxable

No.

Residence requirements

If you are deported you may lose your pension.

Means tested

No.

Earnings rule

None.

Contribution test

None.

Effect on other benefits

You can't get a War Widow's Pension as well as a National Insurance Widow's Pension, but you can get a **Retirement Pension** or other benefit on your own contributions.

The first £5 is ignored for **Housing Benefit** and **Income Support.**

Additions for dependants

£12.00 a week for each child. This continues while the child is in full-time education or apprenticeship or if **disabled** before the age of 16. A parent or other dependant may get a pension at a maximum rate of £1 per week.

Effect of going abroad
None.

Who administers it
War Pensions Office, Norcross, Blackpool, FY5 3TA. Tel. 0253 856123.

Special tips
You may get help with the cost of your child's education and with the cost of a home for a child who gets an allowance. This rent allowance may be up to £20.35.

If your husband dies from wounds inflicted during active service his estate is exempt from inheritance tax.

How to find out more
Books:
Ogus and Barendt's, *The Law of Social Security. Disability Rights Handbook.*

Leaflets: MPL152.

Organisations: War Pensioners Welfare Service, and the Royal British Legion.

War Widow's Pension *see* **War Pensions**

Weather *see* **Fuel**

Wider Opportunities Training *see* **Work, looking for**

Widowed Mother's Allowance

Main conditions

● You are expecting a child of your late husband's

or

● You get **Child Benefit** for a child who is either
   yours and your late husband's, or
   a child your husband was entitled to **Child Benefit** for before his
   death, or

a child of yours by an earlier marriage which ended by your being widowed, if you were living with your late husband when he died.

or

● a person under 19 lives with you who would fit into the previous category, but didn't get **Child Benefit** at the time because he or she was abroad or over 16 when your husband died.

Amount

£41.15 a week if your husband's contribution record is sufficient. If it isn't you may get a reduced rate of benefit. You may also get an earnings related component. *See* **National Insurance** Contributions.

How long does it last

As long as your children qualify you for it.

Taxable

The main benefit is taxable but the increase for children isn't.

Earnings rule

None.

Contribution test

● Your husband must have paid at least 52 times the minimum **National Insurance** Contribution in any tax year before he died, and

● He must have paid contributions for sufficient years out of his working life. The full rule is explained under **Retirement Pension.**

Effect on other benefits

Taken into account in full for all benefits.

Additions for dependants

£8.40 a week for each child.

Special tips

You will probably need to claim **Housing Benefit** or **Income Support** as well. *See* **Single Parents** for more details.

Widows

To get any benefit as a widow you must be married to your husband at the time of his death. You are still entitled if you were separated or if your divorce had not reached the stage of decree absolute. You may be entitled to benefits from your husband's firm as well. Rules for occupational pensions may be different from those explained in this article.

Benefits for widows

	With children	**Without children**
Initially	**Widow's Payment** **Widowed Mother's Allowance**	**Widow's Payment** **Widow's Pension** if over 45 at husband's death
After children cease to qualify if then over 45	**Widow's Pension**	

If your husband died as a result of war then you may qualify for a War Widow's Pension. If he dies from an industrial injury or disease you qualify for widow's benefits without having to pass the normal contribution test.

Other benefits for widows

There are special rules to help widows and widowers qualify for **Invalidity Benefit** if they don't have sufficient **National Insurance** Contributions to get **Sickness Benefit**. A widower must be incapable of work at the time of his wife's death, or within 13 weeks afterwards. A widow gets this help if she does not qualify for a full-rate **Widow's Pension.**

Income Tax for widows

In the year your husband dies and the following tax year you are entitled to a widow's bereavement allowance if your husband was entitled to the married man's allowance. This means that you are taxed at the same rate as a married man. In following years you are taxed as a **single parent** if you have children.

See Inland Revenue leaflet IR23 Income Tax and Widows.

Organisations for widows

CRUSE, the national association for the widowed and their children. 126 Sheen Road, Richmond, Surrey TW9 1UR.

The National Association of Widows, c/o Stafford District Voluntary Service Centre, Chell Road, Stafford ST1 2QA.

Common rules for all widow's benefits

Claims

You should claim on Form BW1 within six months of your husband's death if you have children or within a year if you have none. Otherwise you will lose money unless you can show good cause for the delay. You will need your marriage certificate and your husband's death certificate, but if you don't have them for any reason don't delay in claiming.

Once you have claimed you will be sent forms to claim the other benefits at the right time.

Payment

Normally weekly in advance by order book but can be paid direct into your bank account.

Partners

If you remarry you lose your entitlement to widow's benefits. If you live together with a man as his wife your benefit will stop while you are doing so. For an explanation of what the **DHSS** mean by 'living with a man as his wife' *see* **Partners.**

Effect of going abroad

Benefit continues, but your benefit will not be increased in line with inflation if you do not normally live in Great Britain. It is possible to claim widow's benefits if you are abroad when your husband dies.

Who administers it

DHSS local office.

Appeals

To the Social Security Appeal Tribunal.

How to find out more

Books:
Rights Guide to Non-Means-Tested Social Security Benefits
Ogus and Barendt

Widow's Payment

Main conditions
You must be under 60 when your husband died, or for some reason he was not getting a **Retirement Pension.**

Contribution test
Your husband must have paid at least 25 minimum rate **National Insurance** Contributions before he died.

Amount
A tax-free lump sum of £1000 paid as a giro cheque.

Effect on other benefits
Ignored for **Social Fund** payments for Funeral expenses, so you may be able to claim that too.

Widow's Pension

Main conditions
You must be over 45 but under 65 either when your husband died or when your **Widowed Mother's Allowance** stopped.

Amount
The basic rate is £41.15 a week. You may also receive an earnings related component. *See* **National Insurance.** If you are under 55 when your husband dies or when you cease being entitled to **Widowed Mother's Allowance** you get a reduced rate of benefit. The reduction is 7% for each year you are below 55. So if you are 54 at that time your benefit is £38.27. If you are 45 it is £12.35. The reduction doesn't alter as you get older.

How long does it last
Until retirement.

Taxable
Yes.

Contribution test
The same as **Widowed Mother's Allowance.**

Effect on other benefits
Counts in full for all **means-tested** benefits. You can get **Invalidity Benefit** together with Widow's Pension. *See* **Widows** for more details.

Women

This article is for women who have a **partner** or are married.

Why should the woman claim?

If the woman claims the couple may get more benefit. If you are not sure if you count as a couple *see* **Partner.**

Signing on

Thousands of women miss out on benefit because they don't sign on. If you want a job, sign on. It doesn't matter if your partner is **employed** or **unemployed,** or if you look after **children.**

These are the advantages of signing on:

● You might get **Unemployment Benefit.**
● Your **National Insurance** Contribution will be paid, helping you to get a **Retirement Pension** in your own right, and benefits like **Unemployment, Sickness** and **Invalidity Benefits** in the future.
● You may be able to get free or cheap education, training courses and sports.

If you are over 60 or get benefit because you are incapable of work or getting **Invalid Care Allowance** don't sign on because there is nothing to gain.

See **Unemployed** for details of how to sign on. Don't be put off if you are told you don't need to sign on. It is your right to sign on if you want to.

Income Support

A woman may be able to claim for herself, her **partner** and any **children.**

Why should she claim?

● Sometimes the man may not be able to claim, because he is, for example, a **student.**
● The woman gets the money. The partner who makes the claim gets the benefit. The couple might decide it is better for the woman to manage the money.
● Tax reasons. If the woman gets the benefit without having to sign on, any benefit paid to her is not taxable.

How to claim

Write to your local **DHSS** office. You will need your **partner** to sign the letter as well to show his agreement, if he agrees. If he doesn't agree to you making the claim the DHSS will decide between you.

Family Credit

The woman in a couple can claim **Family Credit** if she works for 24 or more hours a week. **Family Credit** is for people in low paid work with children. If her partner gets **Sickness** or **Unemployment Benefit** she can't claim **Family Credit** until he has been off work for three months. *See* **Family Credit** for more details.

Health Benefits and hospital fares
Free:

- milk and vitamins
- prescriptions
- dental treatment
- help with glasses
- **hospital** fares for patients

Thousands of women don't claim these **Health Benefits.** The woman in the couple can make the claim. You are entitled to them if you have a low income from other benefits or wages. If you are pregnant or have had a baby in the last 12 months you get prescriptions and dental treatment free. *See* **Health Benefits** and **Hospital** for more details.

Retirement Pension
If you are divorced after you have retired and got a full pension your divorce makes no difference. If you don't get a full pension you may be able to use some of your ex-husband's contributions to improve your record. You can also do this if you divorce before you retire, but only for the years you were married. This does not affect your ex-husband's pension, and he need not know about the substitution.

If you are separated but not divorced you will only get a dependant's addition on the basis of your husband's contributions, so if you don't have a pension in your own right it is worth getting divorced.

Other Benefits
If the woman in a couple gets other social security benefits she might be able to claim extra for her children and for her partner. *See* **Dependants.** *See also* **Single Parents.**

Work   *see* **Employed**

Work — Looking for

There are three sorts of help you might be able to get if you are looking for work. They are:

1. Training.
2. Subsidies, for either you or your employer.
3. Travelling expenses, to help you look for work or go to work when you have found a job.

Training

For details of training which will help you find a job contact your local Jobcentre. The main schemes are:

- Wider Opportunities Training. These courses are arranged locally and you may be entitled to a weekly allowance and help with your travelling costs.
- **Job Training Scheme.** These courses are designed to teach you new skills or update your existing skills. You may be entitled to a weekly allowance and help with your travelling costs.
- Access to information technology. These courses are part-time and are held in the evening or at weekends.
- Courses for setting up a business.

Training allowances

If you are awarded an allowance you will get £38 a week, plus £3.55 for your meals. If your fares are more than £4 a week you can claim them back. If you have an adult **dependant** who earns less than £36 a week you can claim an extra £24.70 a week. If you have to live away from home during the course you can claim an extra £40 a week. These allowances are tax free.

If you attend any MSC courses you can claim **Income Support** without having to sign on. Anything from your allowance which you spend on fares will not be counted as part of your income.

Subsidies

Most of the schemes of subsidy are for employers, rather than employees, although there is nothing to stop you suggesting to an employer that he might be able to get a subsidy to help him employ you. Employers can get subsidies to employ people under 18 for low wages (Young Workers Scheme) or set up part-time jobs instead of full-time ones (Job Splitting Scheme). There are also a number of subsidies to encourage employers to take on **disabled** people.

An **unemployed** person can qualify for a Jobstart allowance of £20 a week for six months. You have to take a job where the gross wages are less than £80 a week. The allowance is taxable. You have to have accepted a job before you apply, and acceptance is not automatic. Get leaflets EPL165 (rev) and EPL168 (rev) from the Jobcentre. Jobstart money does not affect **Housing Benefit.**

See also **Enterprise Allowance** if you are thinking of setting up your own business.

Travelling expenses

The Travel to Interview scheme is run by the Jobcentre to encourage unemployed people to look for work in places beyond normal travelling distance from home. You may qualify for a substantial grant towards the cost of moving home if you are successful.

Working, benefits while   *see* **Employed**

Youth Training Scheme

The Youth Training Scheme (YTS) guarantees to provide 2 years of work experience and training for 16-year-old school leavers. A 17-year-old school leaver is eligible for a one year YTS place. **Disabled** people can join a YTS up to the age of 21 and stay on for an extra 3 to 6 months. Your parents' right to claim **Child Benefit** for you ends when you register for your YTS place. If there is no place available for you immediately you get a YTS Bridging Allowance until it is.

Most people on the scheme are taken on as trainees, which means that they have almost no rights. It also means that the payments you get are not liable for **Income Tax** or **National Insurance** Contributions. If you are taken on as an employee you will have similar rights to other people who are **employed.**

You cannot get any benefits for incapacity for work whilst you are on the YTS, but you can claim **Income Support** without having to sign on. You are given credits towards your **National Insurance** Contributions. If you refuse to take up a YTS place or leave it you will not normally be entitled to any **Income Support.**

You get a weekly allowance of £28.50, increased to £35 in the second year. This includes £3 for fares. If your fares are more than this your allowance can be increased to cover the extra costs. If you claim **Income Support** the actual cost of your fares will be disregarded. You should not be asked to work more than 40 hours a week. You are entitled to 1½ days paid holiday for each month you work.

If you are on a YTS you can get a 33% reduction on all normal National Express coach fares, if you buy a card for £2.90 which will last you for a year. Contact your managing agent for details.

You can get more details about YTS from the Jobcentre.

How To...

How To . . . Books
Opening Doors of Opportunity

A major series of self-help paperbacks packed with valuable information on new opportunities in today's fast-changing world. Each of these user-friendly handbooks gives clear up-to-date information and advice, prepared by experts, and complete with checklists for action and self-assessment material. The guides will save you time and money by supplying essential information which is often hard to find.

Helpfully clear layout with illustrations and cartoons, glossary, useful sources, index. Each 215 x 135mm, £4.95 approx.

You can't afford to miss the 'How To . . . series'

How to Get That Job Joan Fletcher
'This book should be mandatory reading for all trainees of YTS/JTS.' *Comlon (LCCI)*
0 7463 0326 2

How to Pass Exams Without Anxiety David Acres
'Should save students many precious hours of revision time.' *Institute of Administrative Accountants*
0 7463 0334 3

How to Live and Work in Australia Laura Veltman
The unique handbook for all those considering employment and residence 'Down Under'.
0 7463 0331 9

How to Live and Work in America Steve Mills
Packed with new ideas on home life, leisure, travel, social and business opportunities.
0 7463 0323 8

How to Help Your Child at School John West-Burnham
Vital information and advice for every concerned parent.
0 7463 0329 7

How to Use A Library Elizabeth King
'The recommended purchase.' *The School Librarian*
0 7463 0317 3

How to Raise Business Finance Peter Ibbetson
'Gives a lucid account of the steps by which a small businessman can substantially strengthen his case.' *The Financial Times*
0 7463 0338 6

Dozens more titles in preparation. For details please contact Dept BPA.

Northcote House Publishers Ltd., Harper & Row House,
Estover Road, Plymouth PL6 7PZ, United Kingdom.
Tel: Plymouth (0752) 705251 Telex: 45635.